HESTER'S
BOOK OF BREAD

Hester van der Walt

HESTER'S
BOOK OF BREAD

Hester van der Walt

modjaji books

Publication © Modjaji Books 2012
Copyright © Hester van der Walt 2012

First published in 2012 by Modjaji Books PTY Ltd
P O Box 385, Athlone, 7760, South Africa
modjaji.books@gmail.com
http://modjaji.book.co.za
www.modjajibooks.co.za

ISBN 978-1-920590-00-0

Cover artwork: Lies Hoogendoorn
Cover design: Life is Awesome Design Studio.
Book design: Life is Awesome Design Studio.
Printed and bound by Mega Digital, Cape Town
Set in Palatino

Dedicated to

Lies & Niël

Monday morning. After the walk with Pixel I start designing a new dress from a Kikoi. My old feet are talking sit down first and draw while Dozi keeps me company with Liewe Lulu in Zulu.

Content

Recipes

1

Searching for the perfect
ciabatta

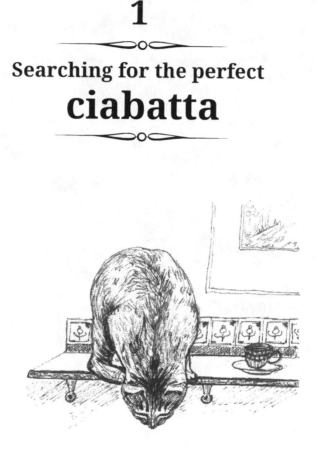

There's bread – and then there's Bread. This is what I realised when I first put my teeth into a true ciabatta, the air-filled Italian loaf named after a slipper. I was on holiday in Florence in the early nineties when I encountered this flat and earthy loaf with its crust like a rugged landscape. As I pulled it apart in my fingers and mopped up the last splashes of sauce from my plate, I knew that a quest had begun. I wanted to bake such bread.

I started paging through recipe books as I searched from one bookshop to the next. Poised nonchalantly at the cookery shelves, my notebook balanced on my bag, I surreptitiously copied down bread recipes. At home I tried them, waiting with excitement to take the loaves from the oven. Ah ... not bad! But the first cut through the crust would tell me every time – this is not the real thing. They all tasted like the homemade bread of my childhood – quite good, but only while still warm.

So my search continued, mostly with the same disappointing result. I discovered that most Italian food books did not include bread recipes at all. Why should they, when there's a good bakery in every neighbourhood?

Then one day I came across a very special book, Nancy Silverton's Breads from the La Brea Bakery. The black and white photographs struck me as both serious and inspiring. This is how she begins: "I don't like ugly bread. The most important thing in bread is the flavor, what you might call the inner beauty of the loaf. In breadmaking looks tell. The more beautiful the loaf, the better it tastes." For the first time I felt that I'd met someone who really shared my passion for bread.

On the flyleaf of my copy I wrote: "May 1997. Desperately seeking the secret of creating the perfect ciabatta."

Silverton is an American and like me, she had always assumed that extraordinary bread is baked only in Europe. Then she started to experiment. Like an acolyte at her feet, I tried slavishly to follow her every instruction. Not easy, because the lay-out of the book is not exactly user-friendly. On top of that, Silverton's book deals exclusively with sourdough bread. Before you can even think of mixing the dough for your first loaf, you have to build up your sourdough starter for a period of fourteen days! Nevertheless, I did not let this deter me. I pressed on with an almost religious fervour, yet for some reason the end result was still disappointing. Was I simply not ready yet, still too busy with other stuff? Or perhaps too anxious?

It was 2001 before another bread book had such a magnetic attraction for me. This was during a period of enormous change in my life. I had just resigned from my job, against the well-meant advice of my colleagues and contrary to every instinct of the older sister's voice in my head. "What are you doing?' she admonished. "Keep going until you're sixty, then at least you'll get a decent pension!" But I was exhausted and had lost all the joy that my once thrilling research work had given me. I wanted out.

One afternoon I drifted into a large bookshop on the Cape Town Waterfront. Inevitably I was drawn to the cookery section, where this title struck me: Artisan Baking Across America by Maggie Glezer. From the cover, a full-colour close-up of a perfect French baguette called out to me. I began to page and to read, and soon I forgot where I was. Time stood still. Eventually I was shaken to my senses when I saw the price on the back cover: R350. Reluctantly I returned the book to the shelf and left the shop. But putting it out of my mind was not so easy, and the next day I was back. "Don't be silly," the sensible sister's voice said. "You're not even getting a salary at the end of this month." But again I sat down with the book and fell under its spell. It was written just for me! Glezer had consulted with artisan bakers for whom bread-making was a vocation and a form of art. She'd adapted their recipes and methods for ordinary people, while still honouring the age-old principle and foundation of bread-making. When I next came back to reality I was already at the till, my credit card swiped and the treasure safely stowed in one of those classy shopping bags.

The book was mine to take home. And that reckless purchase was the best buy of my life. I was burnt out and had lost all my lust for life. That book was the spark that set me alight again.

For the next few weeks all I wanted to do was to bake bread. The first one I tried was the baguette on the front cover, and after that there was no stopping me. Even the Italian bread came out well. The perfect ciabatta at last! There was a huge amount of information, from the different formulae bakers use to design recipes, to the chemistry of combining flour, water and yeast. I revelled in it all. And I marvelled that while the science of fermentation made logical sense on the page, it still failed to penetrate the real alchemy of baking: the miracle that these simple ingredients – water, yeast, flour and salt – can change into living dough between my fingers.

✦

Now, several years later, I make ciabatta every week for the local market in McGregor, and it remains my most popular loaf.

Today our neighbour Pieter is fifty years old. His beloved Suenel has organised a giant celebration. The yard is a sight to behold. Children between the ages of two and eighty-two are playing with a ball on the lawn. Dogs plait their way among the guests' legs. Huge snoek sizzle on the barbecue, five at a time. I have produced thirty ciabatta for the occasion. Over the past weeks I have made extra loaves and hoarded them in my freezer. Here they are now, stacked in a basket next to the generous bowls of salads. The guests are queuing up in a long line.

Etienne, Suenel's brother, is the self-appointed cutter of bread. As the guests dish up he cuts two thick slices of bread, with cheese and a lump of butter for each plate. Later, when everyone is replete after the meal, I find him sitting at the long table on the stoep. He is the centre of attention, gesticulating with his hands as he makes his point. He is wearing a pair of leather shorts and a colourful bandana round his neck. He beckons to me to come and sit in the chair next to him.

"Let me tell you, it was not pure altruism that made me cut those thirty loaves!" His blue eyes are flashing. "No, I wanted to experience the mystery of your bread, I wanted to touch each one of them and get intimate with the crust and the crumb ... I've always dreamt of producing bread with such huge holes!"

I look at him, dumbfounded. The man seems to be describing an orgasm. He is one who can work with his hands, an architect who builds clay and cob houses. While listening to him I remember my own yearning of years ago. How I longed for someone to show me how to do it. I start sharing the secrets of ciabatta dough; wet, very wet dough. After a while I notice that our companions around the table are listening in quiet astonishment. One of the women has been trying to draw Etienne's attention but all he sees now, is bread.

"You see," I explain, "if you have the dough in a bowl, you fold it like this. Nearly like handling a towel that is soaking in the bowl." Around us, people are wide-eyed. "You'll soon notice how the gluten begins to develop and the dough firms up."

"Yes," Etienne nods. "Then it's easier to shape the dough." This is clearly a discussion between two people who are hopelessly in love with bread-making.

Later I walk home to print a copy of my recipe for Etienne. On my way back to the party I hesitate at my backdoor. I remember that our architect had got the recipe for our kitchen's dung floor from Etienne. I open my freezer and take out a Klein Karoo loaf of sourdough. Soul mates are scarce. You don't meet one every day.

✦

Ciabatta Recipe

First, a timeline:

> This recipe requires a firm biga, or starter dough. The starter requires 24 hours to expand fully into a sponge-like consistency. It consist of flour, very little yeast, and cold water which slows down the fermentation.

> The next step is to make the dough

> This is followed by 3 hours of fermentation

> The dough is shaped and left for a further hour to proof.

> Then, at last, the baking period of about 30 minutes.

My favourite recipe is adapted from one I found in Maggie Glezer's Artisan Baking Across America. I have simplified it to suit our local ingredients and conditions. The end result is a lovely loaf filled with huge holes, just perfect for mopping up sauces, or to have with soup or salads. It is lovely for picnics and can be sliced horizontally for sandwiches. For a real South African treat use this dough for stylish roosterkoek, rolls cooked on a barbecue.

If you are fairly new to baking, I suggest you first read Chapter 6 which deals with the equipment and techniques of bread-making. If you don't have scales, I suggest standard measuring cups and spoons.

With good planning you could make the starter dough on a Friday morning, make your dough on Saturday morning, and introduce the ciabatta with a flourish at your lunch time picnic. This recipe yields one kilogram of dough, enough for two large ciabattas or four to six smaller ones.

Starter Dough

¼ teaspoon instant yeast

230 g/ml water

300 g (2 ¼ cups)
white bread flour

15 g (2 tablespoons)
whole wheat flour

15 g (2 tablespoons)
rye flour

185 g/ml cold water

Dissolve the yeast in the 230 g water.

Combine all three types of flour in a mixing bowl.

Add ½ teaspoon of the yeast mixture to the flour. Discard the rest of the yeast mixture.

Add the cold water to the flour and mix, first with a wooden spoon, then with your hand and your dough scraper.

Knead for about 5 minutes or until you have a very firm dough.

Slip the bowl with the dough into a plastic bag. Leave to rise for 24 hours. Choose a cool spot in summer and a sheltered spot in winter. The dough will grow fourfold and has a strong yeast smell when ready.

Dough

325 g (2 ½ cups) white bread flour

1 teaspoon instant yeast

2 ¼ teaspoons salt

345 g/ml water

Fermented starter dough

Mix the flour, salt and yeast.

Cut the starter dough into smaller pieces and add to the flour mixture, together with the water. Combine with a spoon until it forms a rough dough.

Turn the dough out onto your work surface and knead for about 10 minutes. It will be gooey, more like a batter than dough. Use your one hand and the dough scraper in the other, but do not add more flour. The dough should be smooth, still moist and should spread out on the surface.

First Rise and Folding of Dough

Scrape the dough into a large bowl and cover well with plastic. Allow to ferment for 2½ to 3 hours.

During the first hour of fermentation, "lift and fold" the dough three times at 20 minutes intervals, to develop the gluten. Do this as follows: Place a jug with clean water next to your bowl. Use one hand to handle the dough and the other to hold the rim and turn the bowl. Dip your dough hand into the water and insert it under the dough at a point directly opposite you. Lift a portion of the dough, stretch it, bring it towards you and let it fall down in a fold. Repeat this action three more times, turning the bowl through 90 degrees (a quarter of the way) each time, until the dough has been lifted and folded all around. Remember to dip your hand into the water every time to prevent the dough from sticking. You will notice how the lifting and folding firms up the dough.

Cutting, Shaping and Proofing the dough

Flour a dough cloth liberally and make two troughs to receive the dough. Set the cloth aside. (See Chapter 6 for more on proofing cloths).

Sprinkle flour on top of the dough and tip it out onto your surface.

Use a dough scraper to cut the dough into two pieces. (You may prefer to divide the dough into four or six pieces.)

Stretch each piece roughly into a rectangle and fold it loosely into thirds, like a business letter. Handle the dough lightly to avoid deflating it.

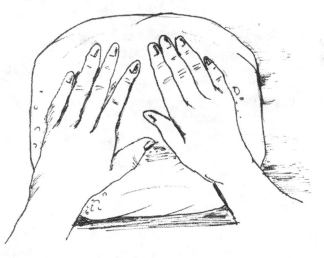

Place each loaf, seam side down, between two folds of the floured dough cloth. Sprinkle the top of the loaf with more flour. Slip the "loaded" dough cloth into a plastic bag.

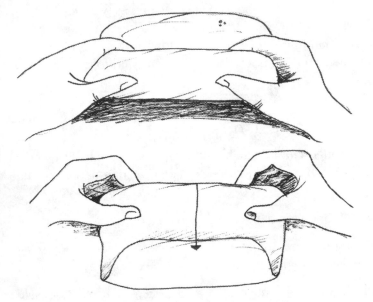

Allow to proof for 45 – 60 minutes.

Baking

Preheat your oven to 230 degrees Celsius. Place an empty baking tin at the bottom of the oven. This will be your steam pan.

Once the loaves are fully proofed, slip each one onto a baking sheet, on top of a piece of parchment paper. Don't be afraid to handle the dough – at this stage it is very forgiving and all dents will correct by themselves.

Using your fingertips, dimple the dough by pressing down to the paper or baking sheet.

Pour one cup of boiling water into the steam pan and close the oven until it has reached the required temperature again.

Place the breads in the oven. **Bake** for approximately 30 minutes, rotating them after 15 minutes to ensure even browning. When done, the breads should be dark brown all around.

Let loaves cool on a rack.

This ciabatta recipe also makes a great focaccia base.

Potato ciabatta

And now, by popular demand, the recipe of my most popular loaf; the potato ciabatta. This beautiful loaf has large air cells and a crisp crust which becomes chewy if you have left over for the next day. Its irresistible flavour comes from the slow rising starter and the addition of mashed potatoes to the dough. The recipe makes one large or two smaller loaves.

Suggested schedule

The night before baking: Make the starter and prepare the mashed potato. The next morning: mix the dough, proof it for about 2 hours and bake it for about 45 minutes.

The starter

¼ teaspoon instant yeast

150 g/ ml water

100 g (2/3 cup) white bread flour

In a measuring jug dissolve the yeast into the water and let it stand for a few minutes. Now add only 60 g / ml of the yeast mixture to the flour and discard the rest.

Mix to incorporate the flour. Let it rest for 10 to 20 minutes before kneading it lightly for about 5 minutes. It should form a sticky dough.

Cover with plastic and leave until doubled and very bubbly. If your kitchen is warm, put it in the fridge after about 3 hours of fermentation. Remove it in the morning I hour before starting the dough.

Preparing the potato

You could do this the night before baking when you make the starter. You will need 85 g or one small potato. Halve the potato and boil it in ample water without salt. Drain and retain the water for later use. Remove the skin and mash the potato, Store in a covered container. You will need about ¼ cup of mashed potato.

Dough

580 g (cups) white bread flour

420 g / ml water, including the potato water

All of the starter

¼ teaspoon instant yeast

15 g (1 tablespoon) sugar or 2 teaspoons honey

60 g mashed potato

15 g (1 tablespoon) salt

Mix the flour and water into a rough, very wet dough in a large bowl. Cover the dough and rest it for 10 to 20 minutes.

Cut the starter up into a few smaller pieces and add to the dough together with the sugar or honey, the yeast, potato and salt and mix everything with a wooden spoon. Moisten your hands and knead the dough until it is smooth, for about 10 minutes. At first it will feel grainy and rubbery, but if you persist it should form a smooth but very wet and sticky dough. Use your dough scraper to help you move it around, but try not to add more flour.

Turning and fermenting the dough

Scrape the dough into a large bowl at least 3 times its size and cover well with plastic wrap. It has to ferment for 3 to 4 hours, or until doubled and filled with large air pockets. During the first hour of fermentation, " lift and turn" the dough three times at 20 minutes intervals to develop the gluten. Do it as follows:

Place a jug with clean water next to your bowl. Use one hand to handle the dough and your other hand to hold the rim of the bowl and to turn the bowl. Dip your dough hand into the water and insert it under the dough at a point directly opposite you. Lift a portion of the dough, stretch it, bring it towards you and let it fall down in a fold. Repeat this action three more times. Every time you turn the bowl a quarter until the dough has been lifted and folded all around. Remember to dip your hand into the water to prevent the dough from sticking to your hand. You will notice how the lifting and folding firms up the dough. Cover and leave the dough for the rest of time, but beware of over fermentation. Alternatively, you could refrigerate it for up to 12 hours.

Dividing, Shaping and Proofing the dough

Remove the dough from the fridge I hour before shaping. Flour a dough cloth liberally and make two troughs to receive the dough Flour the top of the dough and tip it out on your surface.

Use a dough scraper to cut the dough in two in two pieces. (or divide the dough into several 100 - 80 g pieces for potato panini)

Stretch each piece roughly into a rectangle and fold them loosely into thirds, like a business letter. Handle the dough lightly to avoid deflating it.

Place each loaf into a cloth trough and sprinkle with more flour. Slip them into a large plastic bag.

Allow to proof for 1– 1 ½ hours.

Baking

Preheat your oven to 230 *C Place an empty baking tin at the bottom of the oven. When the loaves are fully proofed, slip each one into a baking sheet, or on a piece of parchment paper. Don't be afraid to handle the dough – at this stage it is very forgiving and all dents will correct by themselves. Using your fingertips, dimple the dough pressing to the paper or baking sheet.

Pour one cup of boiling water into the steam pan and close the oven until it reaches the temperature.

Slip the breads into the oven. Bake them for 15 minutes, check and rotate if necessary to ensure even browning. When done the breads should be dark brown all around. Let loaves cool on a rack.

Cousin Focaccia

What is a focaccia? Opinions differ widely, but the general description is of a flat bread with a filling or topping of, for instance, cheese, herbs and olives. Most importantly though, no matter how fancy the filling or the topping, nothing can compensate for a third-rate crust. The above ciabatta recipe will not let you down.

Fillings and toppings

Peter Reinhart's book The Bread Baker's Apprentice gives excellent guidelines for the use of toppings. He distinguishes between toppings that will burn easily and therefore need to be surrounded by dough to protect them, and others that may safely be placed on top.

Toppings such as marinated sun-dried tomatoes, pesto, olives, garlic, fresh herbs, nuts and roasted peppers should be folded into the dough during the shaping stage, before proofing. When you have shaped your dough into a rough rectangle, spread the filling over the entire surface before folding it into thirds.

Moist toppings such as blue cheese, mozzarella and feta can be placed on top of the dough just before baking. Harder cheeses such as Parmesan, pecorino or cheddar are more likely to burn or dry out and should rather be added during the last few minutes of baking, or when the loaves are being rotated.

Herb oil makes a very delicious topping. Reinhart's herb-oil recipe has inspired me to flavour oil with herbs from my own garden. Here's how:

Gently warm a cup of olive oil and add 1/2 a cup of freshly chopped herbs – any combination of basil, parsley, rosemary, thyme, sage and chives. Also add 2 teaspoons salt, 1 teaspoon ground pepper, and 1 tablespoon crushed garlic. Infuse the mixture at a low heat for about 10 minutes. Do not boil. Cool before using, and keep in the fridge for up to two weeks. This oil can be dribbled liberally onto focaccia dough after you have dimpled the dough.

Flatbreads from the Near East and Central Asia are among the earliest breads we know of. Among their descendants -- pittas, Iranian barbaris and chapatis – none are as popular as the delicious ciabatta and focaccia.

2

Ode to the
Oven

Even before meeting him, his wide-brimmed felt hat and canvas backpack caught my attention. At that time my friend Lies and I were managing a small coffee shop in the village. I had left my working life behind and we'd been settled in a rented house in McGregor for a year or so. It was a quiet Sunday afternoon, just before closing time, when I looked up and there he was. A dark-haired open-faced young man busy drawing in the café's book, crayons spread out on the table in front of him. Who is this? I wondered. He seemed completely wrapped up in his own world. Lies placed a coffee on his table and we went outside, leaving him in peace to finish his drawing.

The sun was casting long shadows when he finally ambled down the dusty road to go and find a bed for the night. No car in sight. Had someone dropped him here? Such a mysterious young man. Beautiful too. Perhaps an angel, I thought, and smiled at my own silliness.

As the days went by I discovered that this mysterious young man was Niël Jonker from Oudtshoorn. He had come to McGregor to find clarity, to make sense of his life and seek direction for the future. Watching him move about the village and engage with its people, I knew what was going on in his soul. How would he resolve it – the inevitable tension between free creativity and so-called Reality? Could he make an existence and yet remain true to himself? As the week continued we got to know him better.

What struck me most were his stories and his colourful use of language – his mother's English and the juicy Kannaland Afrikaans of his father. We immediately felt drawn to him, regardless of the barriers of age, and slowly we saw him begin to rekindle his passion for life.

When we met again months later in Oudtshoorn, there was just one topic on Niël's mind: bread. We learnt that he had started to bake, at first from Peter Veldsman's book Cooking with Peter. The process fascinated him so intensely that he was soon baking every day. Then a friend gave him a copy of The Bread Builders. *Hearth Loaves and Masonry Ovens* by Allan Scott, and that was that. He simply had to build an oven. It was mid-winter and his friend's restaurant was closed for alterations, so the timing was ideal for building an oven at the back of the kitchen. They were planning to use it for pizzas, especially during the Klein Karoo festival when queues of hungry people needed to be fed.

Niël was still experimenting and we of course had to go and look at his new obsession. He had already started bread deliveries to a few local restaurants and a handful of privileged friends, so it was a very proud young baker who introduced us to his home-built oven. My first impressions? No way! It seemed like a hell of a lot of work just to get the temperature up to speed. The baker got more fired up than the oven! All very nice, but not for me, I thought.

It was still early days for Niël. He had a lot to learn but his spirits were very high. Just a few short weeks later his bread already looked and tasted like real French boulles.

✦

When we started planning our own house in McGregor, Niël wanted to know whether he could come and build us an oven. By then I had fallen in love with the bread from his oven and I must say I was tempted. It was such a unique offer! How often does the chance arise to have an oven built as part of your yard? But the firing know-how was still veiled in mystery, and I was much older than Niël; would I be able to master a wood oven on my own? In the end my "yes" was based on blind faith and a tiny little fire in my belly. Fortunately Bruno, our architect, was also fired up by the idea and once all the plans had been hatched around our dining room table, my initial misgivings had all been swept away. Except one.

It all sounded terrific, but what would it cost? Could we manage it on our limited budget? Let's have it in black and white, I said to Niël.

On 27 January 2003, the following handwritten fax arrived:

Nomad Oven Crafts
TEL: 0826517414   Address: Anywhere

Esteemed Ladies

It gives me ecstatic pleasure to present you with my quotation for materials required for your oven in McGregor. In this instance, since you are such unsurpassable darlings, there will be no labour costs. Travel costs too will be nil, provided my programme suits you. Cell phone costs will be excluded in exchange for my eating you out of house and home.

May there be peace in your valley until I see you again, probably next Wednesday.

	Price incl VAT	
Steel	52,00	
Vermiculite	193,80	
96 Fire Bricks	12,50	1368,00
125 Red Bricks	4,21	599,93
Foam Shutter	45,00	
Fire & Sairset	190,06	
Total	2448,79	

This quote is for Wednesdays work. The cement, sand, stone, I assume your builders will provide. I also assume that they will build the facade and the chimney. For the second phase I will need a further R 500's worth of small items.

See you on Wednesday,
    Niël.

And so it happened that Niël started to build the oven when the rest of the house was at window height. The builders looked this young guy up and down but soon realised he knew how to wield a trowel. On the very first day already, he and Kaboesie struck up a partnership around the oven's emerging form.

But let me start from scratch. Imagine a structure shaped like a pear, cut in half and placed down on its cut side. The roof is a rounded dome, a bit like a tortoise shell. For perfect radiation and circulation of heat, the proportions within this mystical space have to be absolutely specific and accurate.

Three hundreds years ago the first French immigrants in Quebec built similar ovens. Two anthropologists, Lise Boily and Jean-Francois Blanchette, have taken careful measurements of the inner dimensions of these ovens to determine the principles that informed their design. The height of the roof is crucial – if it is too low, most of the heat will escape through the door, and if it is too high, too much smoke will gather in the vault. Ovens that are rectangular work more efficiently than circular or square ones. The fire is made directly in the belly of the oven, where heat is retained in the walls and the floor. The chimney is situated in the front, outside the oven. Thus air that is sucked into the mouth moves from front to back in a large circular convection, to leave the oven through the same opening where it came in.

In order to build the dome, Niël first made a wooden frame to support the bricks. Kaboesie surveyed the activity from a polite distance. It was only after Niël's dome had collapsed a few times that he edged closer and offered a suggestion. In no time Kaboesie had built up the oven's cavity with sand and stone to create a support for the brick dome. Once the dome was established he simply excavated the sand again. And so it was that Kaboesie became known as a master "arch-angel". Bruno was so inspired that he started inventing arches all over the building site: over the stoep windows; as hatches; and for the pure joy of embellishment he added a festive triple arch for the gate leading to the patio.

When you enter our front gate, you will see two chimneys. The squat middle chimney belongs to our lovely Rubenesque oven.

According to Niël, his ovens have the best looking bums in the world. The oven is the heart of our home. To the back of her is the street and the gate, to the right is the kitchen, to the left the little fountain and Lies's studio, called "Speelonk", and right in front of the oven is the garden. There is no doubt about the gender of this oven. She is decidedly feminine, named Hestia, after the beloved Greek goddess of the hearth. Hestia is not as well known as Astarte and Isis. There are no images of, and hardly any information about her. As far as I could find out her presence is simply indicated with a circle of hearth stones around a fireplace.

Hestia was the daughter of Kronos and Rhea and the sister of Zeus and Hera. As the goddess who tended the sacred fire on Mt Olympus, Hestia was granted the right to maintain her virginity, and thus her independence, forever. She never deserted the home of the gods and thus avoided the endless wars and dramas that engulfed her fellow Olympians. In every citadel or humble home, Hestia provided a refuge to all who sought safety from violence. She is known as the first founder of a true home.

Next to our oven, in a little wall niche, is a simple image of Hestia – two stones, one lightly balanced on the other. The bottom one is a amphibohle while the top onewith the blue sheen is a labradorite. Every week when Lies lights the fire in Hestia's belly, she also lights a candle to the goddess, which she places in the nook. This has become part of our baking ritual.

The first bake in Hestia

The morning is wild with activity around Hestia. Today we are going to try out the oven. Early this morning Niël and I started kneading the dough with the starter that we'd mixed last night at Huis Appelkoos, the cottage we're still renting in the village. While the dough rises in large buckets, we set off down Voortrekker Street to look for firewood, loads of it, because a new oven is hungry and cold. Soon we have gained a little entourage as we are joined by Connie, Carin, Susan, and a group of children who have bunked out of school early.

Making the fire is quite risky as there's still an open ditch between the oven and the partially completed kitchen. The builders regard our activity with sceptical interest, passing quips and comments among themselves.

At last the time comes to scrape the coals from Hestia's glowing belly. When that is done, Niël mops the floor of the oven with an old damp shirt tied to an apricot branch. Then one by one we load the shaped loaves, using a long wooden peel. A chain of human hands passes the loaves from the kitchen counter, over the ditch and into the open mouth. Now close the lid. And wait. We have to be patient for a long twenty minutes before we're allowed to peep.

At last Niël removes the two thorn wood logs that support the oven lid. The corrugated iron plate scrapes over the stone lip. A fiery glow escapes from the mouth. Then I hear myself yelling. Inside, like Daniel and his comrades in the lion's den, sit eight puffed up half-moon loaves. An exact replica of the image on the cover of Artisan Baking. The crusts, black and brown and blonde, smile broadly where I had cut them with a razor blade earlier.

A great cheer goes up. "Ten more minutes," Bread Brother declares and puts the iron cover back over Hestia's mouth. I am floating three feet above the earth. My blood sings. My eyes water. Joy bursts forth from every pore and I let out another victorious whoop.

The next ten minutes have passed in a jubilant haze when I hear the Master Baker of Kamanassie call, "Take up your positions." He holds up his newly made fire scratcher like a wizard's wand. Everything goes quiet. Everyone realises the significance of the moment.

Niël removes the lid and Hestia's glow escapes once more. Right in front of the entrance sits a huge round floor bread, the smiling mother bread. Her smile is the famous grigne of a perfectly slit loaf. The children are big-eyed. The new baker of Hestia is awed, overwhelmed by so much sacredness. Peter Ross is at the front of the line with a wooden tray to receive the loaves as Niël delivers them from the oven amid sighs of admiration. Every loaf is golden brown with a crisp crust: the mother bread, two sourdough whole-wheat loaves, and four whole-wheat batards.

Splendid loaves

Inside the kitchen, cameras flash, corks pop and glasses are filled with red wine. Eyes and faces shine with more than just the heat of the fire. Bruno, the barefoot architect, mounts the podium formed by the vacant kitchen hearth and soars into song. It's an aria from La Boheme. Suenel, our neighbour, brings in a tray with tomatoes and basil from the garden, and a bottle of olive oil. This becomes the first celebratory feast in the kitchen of Pocna – the name of our new house. The Baker of Hestia and the Master Baker of Kamanassie sit on the concrete slab of the unfinished kitchen table. Their cup runneth over. They cut into the mother loaf's crust, then break and share out the bread.

Later it is time to pack up, because Kamanassie is far away and Bread Brother has to get home. Susan and Connie load the loaves into the Mini convertible, and the short trip to Huis Appelkoos becomes a triumphal processional as Connie declares to all and sundry the magnificence of the bread. For a while the entire Voortrekker Street grinds to a halt to admire the bread and share in the magic.

Once home, Hestia's Baker collapses in a heap. Did all of that happen in just one day?

That was Friday the fourteenth of March, two thousand and three: the ritual inauguration of McGregor's wood-fired oven. A few years later our newly-married Bread Brother settled near Baardskeerdersbos, where he continued to paint, bake, and mill his own flour from organic wheat bought directly from farmers nearby. We began to see less of each other then, but our hearts have continued to beat as one and whenever either of us stumbles upon a bread story we always share it. The other day I paged through the old Café drawing book, and there it was – the drawing Niël did in oil pastels on the day we first met him: a cup of black coffee delivered by a pair of hands. The drawing is signed, "Dankie Lies – N".

Here is a recent email from him:

So, I baked again last week and my soul beamed right up above the stratosphere and back again. Gabba went to George for a tutorial and I had a great weekend.

But let me start with Thursday's preparations. The mill (or perhaps the miller) is still on test runs. It stands firmly on four cast-iron legs and sings with joy while it pours forth warm brown flavoursome flour everywhere — onto the floor, my feet, my head, snow white nasal hair. Half a bag of wheat yielded 22 kilograms of flour for the bakery and a further 6 kilos for the chickens, that I swept up from the floor. All of this while the starters are fermenting and wood is being gathered in the blue gum forest under the sheltering arms of mother blue gum and her scaly bark.

Baking day was not so solitary after all because the Miles family joined me. The coals glowed beautifully, and thus the first Strandveld wholewheat baguettes were born and sacrificed straight away, with dripping jam and smacking lips.

Wonderful bread! And best of all, the simplicity. The universe at its best with the minimum of interference.

Thanks for your inspiration and love,

N

✦

Hestia is now several years old and I'm still learning about the unfathomable interplay between wood, fire and dough. The only thing I know for certain is that I will never be in full control of the baking process. Just when I think I have found the perfect balance, or know exactly what kind of oven yields what type of loaf in what season, Life bowls me out for a duck. The truth is, it is impossible to estimate Hestia's temperature. Bread writers all have their own little devices. Some suggest tossing in a handful of flour; if it burns black within a given number of seconds, the oven is still too hot. Another suggestion is to see how long you can keep your hand inside without burning. I have concluded that these theories are worth very little. What complicates matters further is that the heat which is stored in the brickwork of the oven is released gradually, depending on how much is being absorbed by the contents of the oven. For instance, the wetter the dough, the faster the oven cools down. Thus the temperature is never constant. I have often made the mistake of leaving two or three loaves to brown just a little more, only to discover them burnt to cinders a few minutes later. Much better to remove the loaves and return them later on during the bake, when the oven is cooler.

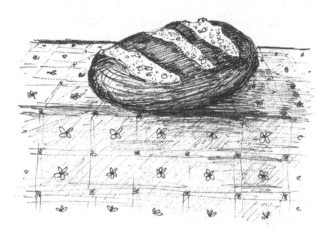

Ovens of Yore

All this pondering about ovens got me to thinking about our grandmothers and the ovens they would have used in the old days. So on a day in late January, when the weather prophet has forecast a hot 35 degrees Celsius, I visit Kleinplasie, the open-air museum near Worcester. My aim is to look at their wood-burning oven, a replica of the type in use on every farm before the advent of the coal stove and the electric oven.

The house at Kleinplasie is based on the original homestead at Melkhoutfontein near Stilbaai. Its low lime-washed walls, small windows and thatched roof remind me of Poena, but as I enter the dark kitchen I am instantly grateful that our own architect had had the know-how to conjure more light.

My tour begins at the hundred-and-fifty-year-old winnowing machine, which also proves the highlight of my visit. The cedar wood box with its hand crank reminds me of a Dutch street organ. Wheat kernels are thrown in at the top, from where they fall onto a set of sieves. As Richard Titus turns the crank, the sieves begin to shake to and fro. The entire machine shudders. Sticks and husks are blown away by the breeze while the clean wheat drops neatly into the lower drawer. Next the wheat is thrown onto the sorting table where Richard removes small stones and other remaining impurities by hand.

The water mill next door is turned by a cedar wheel donated by the farm Dwarsrivier in the Clanwilliam district. Here I watch the ground flour slowly drop into a linen bag, ready for the bake.

Now on to the oven. The baker is Freda Bastiaan. She has stacked her dough-filled baking tins in the fireplace to keep warm. Freda tells me that she started kneading in the wooden trough at eight this morning. Once the dough began to rise she put it into tins. This was a scant two hours ago and the dough is already puffed above the rims of the tins. I imagine that our grandmothers would have kneaded the night before, for the dough to have a slower rise. Freda's bread is almost certainly based on a modern recipe using instant commercial yeast. Oh well, perhaps I'm expecting too much from a "living museum".

By now the men have raked the hot coals from the oven, in preparation for the bake. I'm relieved for Freda's sake, because the oven door is scarcely at knee height, definitely not easy on the back. Could our grannies have been so short? The oven is built on a low platform of stone and concrete. The floor and the thin walls consist of brick and mortar. The oven door is wider than Hestia's and the inside space much larger. The overall shape is square rather than oval. There is no chimney, just a hole high up in the rear wall for smoke to escape. During the bake this hole is covered with a metal plate.

This entire design is so different from the European and Canadian models on which Hestia is based. I wonder about this. Perhaps our African forbears were less concerned to preserve heat, or perhaps they had more than enough firewood. I have been told that they often made an instant fire by burning a dry Karoo bush in-between batches.

I help Freda carry the eight bread tins from the kitchen. She tests the heat – "If I can hold my hand inside to the count of ten, I know the oven is ready" – then shoves the tins into the oven with her bare hand and a short stick. She places the tins in the front of the oven where the fire was raked out earlier. "Now I know that my bread will be ready in an hour," she declares. Then she confirms my assumption that there is enough heat for only a single batch. "If we want to bake more bread, we'll have to make another fire."

Later, as I leave Kleinplasie, I can't help feeling a bit disappointed. Everything I've seen looks a bit tired and unkempt. Could it be that the museum had some earlier charm which has lately gone to seed? What concerns me most, though, is the lack of attention to authentic detail like the fermentation of dough. Where are the true sourdough yeast recipes of our foremothers? And where are the home-grown mosbolletjies (must-buns), especially now during the harvest season? Surely wheat that is stone-milled to golden perfection deserves more authentic care than the shortcut of commercial yeast and a fast-rising process?

Whatever the case may be, long live home baking in the wood-fired oven, in whatever shape or form.

Who is this little woman looking at me from the mirror? Do I know her? What's going on inside her? Is she happy? Why?

She thinks about creating and then she draws herself.

3

The
Fire Maker

"Are you the baker?"

"No, I'm the stoker. But I was born with the aroma of bread in the air. My father was a baker."

This is how Lies chats to people at the market while she sells bread. Her father, Gijs Hoogendoorn, was a highly skilled baker of bread and confectionary with his own bakery in Van der Mark Street in Utrecht. When Lies took me to her birthplace some years ago she couldn't believe how small and cramped it seemed. The shop with its display window was still on the corner. Just behind it used to be a small living room and two tiny bedrooms. There she was born on a beautiful morning in August, while in the midst of all the to-do, money was stolen from the cash drawer.

After the destruction of World War II, the Hoogendoorns, like so many Dutch people, decided to make a fresh start in South Africa. With his bakery equipment as their key to the future, Gijs, his wife and their three children travelled here by boat in 1951. In his pocket was a

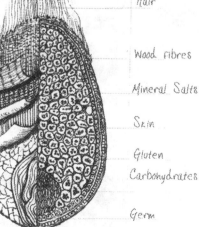

Hair

Wood Fibres

Mineral Salts

Skin

Gluten
Carbohydrates

Germ

Cross section of a grain of wheat as shown in "Het Nieuwe Handboek voor de Broodbakkerij" by Quidam.

temporary permit allowing him to work in Meneer Kritzinger's bakery in Fouriesburg.

The sixteen-year-old Lies had to help her father to make spans, the Dutch term for starter dough. On Sunday afternoons she and her brother would go to the bakery to mix flour and yeast, to provide Oom Gijs with an active sponge from which to start his dough early the next morning. This was Lies's only experience with bread-making. Later on she also assisted with decorating wedding cakes and with bread sales, wrapping each loaf in a rectangular strip of white paper. When business was slow she passed the time by drawing portraits of clients and passers-by on the wrappers.

One day, shortly after I'd become enthused about baking, Lies was sorting out books when she came upon one of her father's old bread books. It was covered in brown linen with the title printed in gold: Het Nieuwe Handboek voor de Broodbakkerij door "Quidam". Uitgave van de NV Uitgevers – Maatschappij AE Kluver – Deventer.

Fouriesburg 1951

I couldn't help wondering why the so-called Quidam would have used a pseudonym to publish his New Handbook for Bread Baking. In the introduction he writes: "Subject literature for the Dutch bakery has been scant up to now, in 1930." He cautions: "First class bakers are few and far between, and those that are around will tell you, even at a ripe old age, that they are still learning every day."

The book had clearly been well used but the pages were still intact. The cover was slightly loose and the pages bear sure signs of little hands drawing pencil lines. I imagine it was often left open on the kitchen table where the Hoogendoorn children played. Did Oom Gijs consult the book for recipes to try out the next day?

On page one there is a fine line drawing of a giant wheat kernel in cross section. This is followed by a discussion of brown bread which, according to a certain Doctor TR Allison, provides "the best food for humanity". Nearly every page is illustrated with a black and white photograph, often hardly decipherable. Where the image is poor, Quidam offers an apology, followed by additional explanation to compensate for the shortcoming. Simple line drawings explain complex processes, such as the making of sugar butterflies. "Luxurious plaiting" takes up an entire chapter. Here you can learn to plait loaves with four or even six dough strands.

The actual recipes are not of much practical use to a small baker like me, since they mostly require about 100 kilograms of flour. I have nevertheless spent many pleasant hours in Mijnheer Quidam's company, savouring both his knowledge about bread and his charmingly archaic language.

Once I started baking for clients, Lies gave me plenty of encouragement but she preferred to stay in the background. She helped me design pamphlets and plan my first marketing efforts. This was my first experience at trying to sell something that I had produced. How do you estimate the cost of an oven-baked loaf of bread? How can you justify it, when you consider the low cost of factory bread? Yes, Lies had to admonish me constantly, but yours is not factory bread. Remember that your product is real artisan bread.

✦

When the day came for us to use our newly-built oven for the first big bake, I again noticed that Lies was hanging back. Niël had shown both of us how to fire the oven and I had hoped that she would be the one to take on this part of the job, but now I suddenly realised how sceptical she was about the whole operation. The amount of dough alone was enough to scare anyone – bowl upon bowl of dough covered every available surface of the little kitchen in Apricot Cottage, where we were still living at the time. I had to transport the bowls and all my equipment to Poena, where the kitchen's dung floor was still too damp for use. There I had to weigh and shape the dough on the covered stoep.

I had a knot in my stomach as I started the fire, trying to remember all Niël's instructions. It was not easy. Friends Johann and Seamus helped me to scratch the coals from the oven. Thankfully the bread came out beautifully that day, but that was pure grace, because there had been no system at all. The first day's loaves were born of sheer chaos.

We have come a long way since then and I am pleased to report that Lies has become the official stoker after all. In the end she had to admit that she is in love with every kind of fire: hearth fires, candles, campfires, and yes, the fire in the bread oven as well. Two years down the line she has mastered Hestia in her own unique and accomplished way. Her motto for every batch is, "Four hours of fire!" She knows every wood seller in the village – the trustworthy ones and the rogues – and she regularly orders 500 to 1000 pieces of exotic wood such as blue gum or Port Jackson.

"Peace in every step," is the key message of Thich Nhat Hahn, the beloved Vietnamese Zen master. He espouses the principle of mindfulness, whereby every aspect of daily living becomes an opportunity to meditate. Through the mindful use of each piece of baking equipment, for instance, bread-making becomes a meditation in action. Thich Nhat Hahn describes how he learned to cut grass with a sickle, something that is only possible if you coordinate every movement of your body with your breathing. If you synchronise breath with action you don't tire easily. Furthermore, if you live the moment to the fullest and are not in a hurry to get the work done, the interplay between wood and hand, fire and oven becomes a unity that nourishes the soul. The same applies to the interplay between the baker and the stoker, as the readiness of the dough and the readiness of the oven need to coincide.

Industrial bakers use proofing ovens to manipulate the temperature of the dough, ensuring that the dough is ripe when the oven is ready. At Poena we achieve the same result through practised estimation and finely tuned cooperation.

Because it is nearly impossible to accurately determine the oven's temperature, the process of baking remains a great adventure. We are always caught between two extremes: the oven is either so hot that the first loaves burn, or the temperature is perfect at the start but too cool to get the final loaves done. We have learnt that it is better to risk the early loaves. Thus Lies fires the oven for four whole hours, and we devise all manner of clever tricks to protect the first loaves against burning, such as placing them on baking tins and covering them with tin foil during their final minutes of baking.

Lies records every bake. Here is an excerpt from the Bread Journal, a notebook filled with the joys and woes of our baking years:

3 June 2003, 1 pm.

Two focaccias out   the first covered with scorched black blisters. The Klein Karoo's are in. I could do with a Frangelica now: the oven is hot, my body is on fire. But first the Klein Karoo sourdoughs have to bake. There goes the alarm. Take a quick look. Watching them with an eagle eye.

We bake. We live. We're in wonder. Such is the quality of life when I look around me, and we look at each other.

On 22 July 2005 she records the number of loaves.

Order of baking:
2 × Focaccia
2 trays epi baguettes
rye bread
karoo 9
karoo 9
karoo 6 and 6 raisin bread
= 7 bakes

Lies uses various strategies to keep Hestia happy. Sometimes the flames just seem to fall away, as if the oven has gulped them up in a spiteful mood. All that is left is a heap of pitch black smouldering logs. This is bad for the oven. Over time it could prevent the even spread of heat, leading to so-called "cool spots". Lies responds by feeding the oven a few pieces of oiled baking paper and within seconds the flames leap up to lick the oven's palate again. At times like this I hear her call, "If you want to see something beautiful you'd better come right now!" The spectacle never fails to amaze her.

With every bake we wonder whether we will have enough heat. Of course we could finish the last loaves in the electric oven, but for Lies this feels like a personal insult. Take last week as a case in point. I realised that the large loaves were taking unusually long to get brown. Well ... what now? We still had nine loaves to go, but I didn't say a word. Later on, while turning the bread, the following dialogue took place.

Hester: "I'm not saying anything, but I see what I see".

Lies: "Go on, what do you want to say?"

Hester: "Same thing the guy said who had to look after the old lady's parrot: No Madam, that I cannot say!"

A fit of laughter overcame us – the kind that can only beset you when you're dead tired after hours of physical work. It descends upon you like a blessed relief, making you forget all about your painful back and shoulders.

Then Lies gets serious again. "What do you mean?" But I know she knows what I mean. "No, Ma'am, that I cannot say," I tease her.

In the end all the day's bread was successfully baked and we had enough heat to roast vegetables and cook an iron potjie full of bean soup.

What more can I say? This oven remains a mystery.

After reading this chapter for the first time, Lies told me why she had been so hesitant to get involved with the baking. When she was a child she saw how hard her parents worked in the bakery. There was little time left for the children. Oom Gijs started at four in the morning and Tante Corry was in the shop all day. Lies remembers these as hard times. Work problems were discussed at home, often in raised voices, because her father was passionate about his bread. Sometimes her mother made mistakes; little wonder, seeing as she also had to care for her young family. To make things worse, this was during the war and Utrecht was under siege by the German army. Fearful times for a little girl who observed everything with wide eyes, and decided that she would never choose a life like this when she grew up!

4

Wood and
Fire

Now we get to the wood stories. Wood is absolutely indispensable; without it we could not bake in Hestia. Yesterday Paul the Potter dropped in to check on our wood. Lies proudly showed him the pile that Moos brings her every week. Lovely stuff that he sells us for fifteen rand a bag. Lies has a special relationship with Moos. They have become quite close over the past six months. A rough diamond, she admits, but you can always bank on him.

But Lies is in for a surprise. Paul needs to examine just one piece of her wood to gather all the evidence he needs: this is his wood, stolen from the woodpile next to his kiln. Not just any wood, mind you, but wood that's been dried over four years to fire his delicate pots! Wood that he orders by the bakkie-load. Wood that is cut with special tools to fit the size of his kiln. Over the past weeks he'd begun to notice a steady decline in his stock. Since we're the only other people in the village who use wood during the summer, he had come here to check. Et voilá, here was the evidence!

Lies is shattered. Moos the Fire Woman's Woodman, is clearly in deep trouble.

"What are we going to do?" she asks.

"I'm reporting him to the police," says Paul. "They have to sort this out. And it's better that way," he adds, "because if I caught him, I'd break his neck."

Paul is livid. I can already picture the headlines: "Murder in

Peaceful Retreat Village"; "White on Black Violence in the Karoo."

After Paul has left, Lies and I reflect on our discovery. I should have trusted my gut feel – from the start I'd had my doubts about Moos but I'd left all the negotiations to Lies. Her faith in the inherent goodness of human nature has taken a hard knock.

"But I've often seen him gathering wood in the krans. With my own eyes …," says Lies.

"Yes," I reply, "but maybe he only steals occasionally, like when it's very hot. Who wants to go so far to chop wood if the neighbours have a huge pile ready? Let's redistribute it a bit, he thinks. And for such entrepreneurship I surely deserve fifteen Rand!"

Much later I see that Lies is still deep in thought. About Moos. About her misplaced trust. About her broken trust. And about the need to adjust her view of humanity to accommodate her much admired, now tarnished wood dealer.

I remember Bread Brother Niël's gift with words and try to cheer her up in similar vein:

> *"May every sly visitor to your pure innocence never harm your trust. May the Karoo summer breezes caress your body like millions of kisses; and may no brush remain dry while you still have stories to share."*

✦

It is a few months later and our last bake has been really difficult. The new batch of wood that Trevor had stacked in neat rows next to the oven looked really promising. Red blue gum sticks cut up in foot-long lengths. But I hear Lies muttering and while I weigh the dough I can see her struggling with the fire. The wood is not dry enough and when she tries to spread the fire to the back of the oven, the flames die down. She redoubles her efforts with smaller twigs but it remains an uphill battle.

When it is time to bake, Lies scrapes the coals to the mouth of the oven with her steel scraper and I shovel them out with a spade. We work in unison, as though sweeping up dust with a broom and pan. I tip the coals into the ash hole under the oven. Today I count twelve shovels of coal, much more than usual. Lies mops the oven floor and we load the first focaccias on baking tins. We set the timer for four minutes.

After six minutes the bread is still pale. We look at each other. We don't say a word, but we both know that this spells trouble. The oven is not warm enough and there are eighty lumps of dough back in the kitchen, each in a different stage of readiness.

Today our neighbour's son, Sage, is here to see what we are doing. He is eight years old and receives home schooling. His mother Susan tells us that he's been dying to bake bread. As his name indicates, he belongs to the new generation of wise children. He wants to know why we are so worried. We don't really want to name the problem yet. The loaves are slowly browning, but we've definitely got a problem on our hands.

One hour later the focaccias are finally done, followed by the first batch of larger breads. The electric oven is on and I start to bake the white loaves, four at a time. And so we limp through the day, from one oven to the other, the large cool Hestia and the small hot Bosch. Lies's mood sinks lower and lower. She thinks it is all her fault; she should have read the signs and kept the fire going for much longer. The vault of the oven requires bright flames but today the wood merely smouldered. But there is nothing to be done and we have shifted into coping mode: manage the heat that we've got; bake certain loaves first; put others back into the fridge to retard the fermentation.

On an average baking day the full session takes about three hours. Today the entire process, in both ovens, takes nearly five. At five o'clock we're finally done. The kitchen receives a quick wipe before we rush off to Temenos to report for a weekend retreat with Pat Hattingh.

Contemplation has become part of the rhythm of our lives. It is similar to Thich Nhat Hahn's practice of mindfulness: a time to turn to the bread of life. After the long hours spent on my feet it is pure bliss to simply sit down.

Pat radiates peace. His eyes seem to probe one's inner being. Unlike many esoteric seekers I've known, this man exudes simplicity. Today he wears light brown corduroys and a green jersey. He has been following the path of advaita for the past thirty years. Advaita is a Sanskrit word meaning "not two, but one". Pat's teacher was a follower of Ramana Maharshi, the Indian sage who always returned to one question only: Who am I? The more one explores this question, the more one appreciates the miracle of one's existence.

From childhood we are conditioned to take on a particular identity, and as we grow up we adopt multiple roles, hiding ourselves behind several masks. I am a woman, Afrikaans speaking, a nurse, a sister and a daughter, a student, a scientist, a lover and a baker. But who am I in essence? Is there an end to these external forms, and where do I find the deepest kernel of my being? Do I extend beyond my body, and what happens to me after death?

Pat leads groups on this kind of self-enquiry, a journey on which I am just starting out but which already fills me with wonder. Where do I end and where do you begin? What about my connectedness with the loaf of bread and the ear of wheat and the drop of rain?

Pat refers to his meditation technique as "dissolving". Its aim is to still the mind and allow the self to dissolve in the present moment. To avoid any sense of disorientation or anxiety he suggests that we anchor ourselves in the physical presence in our hands and the sensations they perceive. Whenever our thoughts threaten to take flight we return to the feeling in our hands.

This is a simple yet challenging instruction. I sit quietly and feel the tensions of the day seep away. The back of my left hand lightly rests in my right palm. A warm glow spreads into my fingers and surrounds my hands. Shoulders and neck relax. A dog barks in the distance. The hadedas scream overhead. While I remain aware of events out there in the world, my primary awareness is here, in my hands, these hands which are still at last, after all the busyness of the day.

Open. To be filled again and again.

✦

The next Tuesday Esau Fourie, our gardener, chops some of the red blue gum logs into smaller pieces. He stacks the kindling next to the oven, ready for Friday's fire. Lies seems confident that all problems are behind us. She starts the fire while I weigh the dough. Today we expect a group of children from the local Waldorf School to visit our bakery.

In no time, I pick up signs of trouble at the oven. Lies struggles with pieces of cardboard and strips of newspaper.

"Go and check next door at Pieter's fire place," I suggest.

Pieter always has lots of wood. He has been chopping up a dead oak tree over a period of some months. After a few minutes Lies returns with handfuls of twigs and bark and begins to rekindle the fire. As I watch her trying in vain again to feed the hungry oven, I feel a mighty surge in my belly. This pussyfooting is never going to do the trick! We need some bigger action here. Pushing a wheelbarrow has never been my forte but I grasp its two handles, tip out its contents, swivel the wheel around with amazing ease, and there I go, back-to-front over the water furrow and on into the neighbour's yard. At Pieter's braai I fill up with dry oak logs and within minutes I am back with my load.

The fire greedily swallows the dry wood and Lies assures me that all is well now. The next moment we are confronted by six little big-eyed faces. Oona, their teacher, tells us that this term they are learning all about farming and growing vegetables. Last week they visited a local dairy to watch how cows are milked and cheese is made. I give each child fifty grams of dough which they shape into round rolls. They arrange their balls of dough on a baking sheet to form a geometric flower shape. Meanwhile Lies tells them all about the fire, which by now, thank you very much, is burning away happily.

While the oven heats up the children go off to make butter. When they return – much sooner than we'd expected – Lies scrapes out the coals. We anticipate that the oven will still be too hot for the rolls, so I switch on the electric oven. Great expectations all round. Little helping hands everywhere. The focaccias go in first to absorb Hestia's fiercest heat. When we check after five minutes, I swear under my breath. Pale. Far too pale! We keep our poise in the presence of the children, but the gods hear our grumbles. OK, the oven is warmer than last week, but still far from what we are used to.

We end up with yet another bake that requires two ovens and several more hours. How hard it is to maintain one's equanimity – in good times and in bad! Friends drop in to congratulate Lies on her birthday. We chat over bread and coffee and this helps to ease some of our disappointment. But I promise myself, next week I will find dry wood. As the Afrikaans idiom goes, a jackal may be caught twice in the same trap, but definitely not thrice!

The experience makes me think about the difference between Lies and me. She tends to be more meek and long-suffering, more inclined to wait and be patient, while I am more likely to step in, to intervene – and sometimes to over-react. Have I got this right? Is this how she sees it?

The next day at breakfast I ask Lies what she thinks.

"You're right," she says. "Remember all those big decisions you've taken? Siloam, Manchester …"

I think this over before I respond. I'd been referring to smaller, everyday events and responses, but she's right, I am impulsive, more likely to take big risks. She needs more time before taking decisions. Is this a sign of anxiety? No, in many areas of life she is much more thorough and decisive than I am. Deurtastend. I like this Afrikaans word. To "feel through". It conjures up an image of hands that carefully feel their way towards suitable action.

One area that Lies "feels through" expertly is our bakery's admin and finances. She sees to it that bills are paid on time. She deals with complex forms and sends heartfelt letters to traffic authorities to plead for leniency with our fines!

During our discussion I am reminded of Lies's fearless way with people. She approaches everyone in an honest, direct manner. She has no pretences and people know where they stand with her; whether she likes them or not, and whether she agrees or disagrees with them. She goes straight to the heart of a matter, like a warm knife slipping through butter. I, on the other hand, tend to be overly cautious in case I hurt someone's feelings. But perhaps the truth lies deeper than this – in reality I'm shit scared to expose myself and risk being rejected by others.

Oh, to be simply honest and to let go of all the little ego games. Is it really possible? The advice of my bald-headed friend, Johann, is to be brave enough to risk disappointment; that is where the greatest growth lies.

Enough philosophising. Let's go in search of dry wood!

✦

Paul the Potter, the guy who came looking for his stolen wood, lives further up Breë Street. The De Jongs' speciality is their wood-fired pots. He builds large wheel-crafted pots while his partner, Nina, makes hand-built tea pots and home ware.

The De Jongs are well known for their giant kiln, which accommodates dozens of pots in multiple chambers. The kiln is equipped with special fire chambers where the fire can be stoked for days before and during the firing process. The mouth is packed with numbered fire bricks, which in turn are sealed with a clay mixture to prevent leakage of smoke and soot. Potters come from all over the country to fire their pots during the De Jongs' famous pottery jamborees.

Today I visit Paul to ask his advice about our wood problem. Behind the kilns, well-stocked wood piles are neatly stacked. I secretly hope that he will suggest swapping some of his dry wood for our damp logs. Paul needs very little time to assess a sample of Trevor's blue gum wood. He is a compactly built man of few words and great presence.

"This is green wood," he declares.

"How do you know that?" I ask, keen to learn from the master.

He points to the annual rings in the cut end of the wood. "This ring shows you this season's growth. Another clue, if the bark is still solidly fixed to the wood, you can be sure that it is still wet."

Paul gives me a guided tour of his wood archives. Wood of all lengths and thicknesses are neatly stacked. The colour of the wood differs according to age. Grey wood is three years old while red and yellow wood is still damp. To cut wood expertly is an art, Paul explains. It takes practice and much care.

"I can no longer do it these days. It gives me shooting pains up my arms and in my wrists. My hands are used to working with the softness of the clay. I have to use the right wood in order to produce quality pots, otherwise there will be a weak link in the process. But I have to rely on other woodcutters. The problem is that chopping wood is one way to make a fast buck, especially if the chopper needs weekend money. In such circumstances he's going to pay little attention to the quality of the wood or the way it is split."

We are fortunate to live in an area where exotic wood needs to be cut down in the interest of nature conservation. Paul selects his wood merchants with much care and he constantly trains them to master the art of wood-making. He orders large loads at a time.

These are then chopped and stored according to date and size. He is a real artisan who loves his work and respects all the elements that combine to form the end product, be it a raku vase, fragile as an egg shell, or a sturdy planter for a rugged aloe.

Paul once showed us a photograph of a fully stacked oven, the vault of its inner chamber filled with earthenware urns. "It looks like a temple," Lies whispered.

"It is a temple," was Paul's solemn reply.

This afternoon we asked Esau to remove all the damp wood from near the oven. He stacked it against the reed shed to dry in the sun. We may be able to use it a few months from now. Meanwhile wood arrives from far and near. Word has gone out on the dorp's informal chatter line. Our neighbour Suenel happens to have some "projection" (Port Jackson) that a friend had brought from his farm for a braai. Nice and dry. Paul de Jong's right-hand man has promised us a load before the weekend.

We still have to give Trevor, the dealer in damp wood, a good talking to, but that can wait. Our first job is to sort and stack our new collection of wood.

5

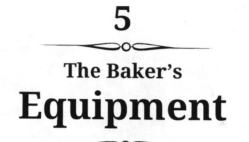

The Baker's
Equipment

Spring is nearly here but a delicate layer of snow dusts the Riviersonderend Mountains like finely sifted flour. I am writing on the patio in front of the oven, at the table that receives the loaves as they are peeled out of the oven. The table with its steel legs and fake marble melamine top was a gift from my cousin Carin, and dates from the fifties. On baking days Lies arranges an eclectic mix of cooling racks on the table. Some of these specimens are badly bent but still perfectly suited for the job. We have collected them from various junk shops in neighbouring towns. We also use an old garden table for the same purpose. Lies places the tables a few feet apart and bridges the gap between them with a few oak planks to give us extra space for cooling the bread. The oak planks were once wine barrels. Dark red stains on the wood tell stories of their previous life. We collected these free of charge from a carpenter's scrap yard in Robertson.

I always loved snooping around in Cape Town's second hand stores in Long Street, Church Street and Kloof Street. Lately the Breede River Valley is my hunting ground. In Robertson the Van Tonder brothers own two of my favourite shops. Kleinboet stocks high class junk sourced at auctions in the area. There is a wide choice of beautifully crafted oak and Oregon pine furniture: wardrobes, chests and chairs. The kitchen section is my favourite haunt. He keeps a selection of best porcelain ware, such as cups, plates and serving dishes, ever so slightly cracked. And don't tell anyone about his enamel ware and granny cake tins! But the best bargains of all are in his attic: old wooden apricot crates that can be turned into rustic bookshelves.

Ouboet Eben runs the large junk shop next door. Gird your loins; for this expedition you'll need all your strength. Row upon row of shelves, sorted more or less into plastics, glass, porcelain, aluminium and linen. Room upon room of furniture from every era, topped with layers of equally historic dust.

In this shop I have found quite a few baking tins and cooling racks. My most exciting buy was a galvanised iron kneading bucket from the fifties. It has a dough hook that can be operated by hand, much like a churn. (See illustration on p .) The bucket can be clamped to a table-top and the instructions are engraved on the lid. First put in water, followed by flour, salt and yeast. Then you start turning the handle. It is easy to begin with, but as the dough starts to form it gets harder to turn the hook. I made good use of this implement when I first started to take bread orders, but after a while I had to admit that cleaning the bucket and its loose parts was not really worth the effort.

The amazing thing is how one learns to improvise. My beloved bread books all mention the use of French bannetons. These baskets made from plaited willow and cane support individual loaves of dough during the proofing stage. They act like perfect moulds and when the dough is turned out each loaf is imprinted with the attractive coil marks of the wood. I once came across these imported baskets in a Cape Town speciality store. My excitement soon turned to disbelief when the cashier informed me of the price. One hundred and eighty rand each! Crazy! I now have a collection of locally made baskets, mostly sourced from Van Tonder's shelves and formerly used as bread baskets in hotels and restaurants.

My pride and joy, though, are the four real bannetons bought for the princely sum of four rand each! They were spotted by Lies on a pavement one morning during a leisurely stroll along Kalk Bay's second-hand tourist-trap boutiques. She had to examine them carefully as they were obscured under a thick layer of old dough and mildew, but viola, they turned out to be the real thing! Having carefully cleaned and aired them in the Karoo sun, we use them every week for proofing rye loaves.

What other equipment does a baker need? Those in the know talk about couches. French again, of course, for lengths of coarsely woven linen. They serve the same purpose as the baskets – to support the shaped loaves during their second rising. Couches are particularly useful for French baguettes. The cloth is folded in deep concertina pleats and generously dusted with flour before the rolls of dough are placed between the  pleats. Like babies in their blankets. Once again improvisation has had to save the day, and I have ended up with a basket full of my own dough cloths. Thick cotton dish cloths, the type with a woven pattern, work perfectly. Unbleached cotton too. Lies has made a special couche for baguettes from an old winter sheet, folded and stitched into a metre long rectangle. In one corner she stitched its name in large letters: Koes, an Afrikaans pun on couche.

It is said that real bakers never wash their couches. The yeast spores that remain in the fabric contribute to the rich and complex flavour of the bread. Usually I dry my bread cloths in the sun before folding and storing them – but I do give them an occasional wash!

While on the topic of French terminology, another word that regularly appears in my bread books is lamé, a special blade that is used to cut or score the shaped dough before it enters the oven. These cuts have more than one purpose. They are decorative and bakers tend to have their own signature cuts, but the real purpose is to prevent the crust from bursting during the final rise, also known as oven spring. In some cases loaves are cut with scissors.

The lamé is nothing other than an old-fashioned razor: a single-edged blade attached to a stick. I believe some men still prefer these to the more conventional modern razors. I have tried using a sharp knife, but with little success. Towards the end of the proofing stage the skin of the dough is very tender and any pressure causes it to collapse and wrinkle.

Even an expedition to the back streets of Salt River, in search of a mythical old-world barber who might still be using this primitive tool, proved in vain. I had just resigned myself to using a pair of scissors when Bread Brother Niël appeared one day with a secretive smile and bearing a mysterious little black box.

"Guess what. I've discovered a real lamé!"

Where? I wanted to know.

"Oh, I stumbled on a website with all sorts of baking stuff, so I ordered us each one."

I lifted the lid of the rectangular black box. Inside I saw a silver coloured hand piece, a packet of Minora blades, and a small scroll of paper.

Niël was beaming. "It's easy!" he said. "You just fit a blade to the hand piece. But don't worry, the instructions are quite clear."

I opened the piece of paper. It was covered in fancy script. "The Original Le Sliceur," it declared. "All instructions to be read with a Strong French Accent."

I go on reading, absolutely amazed.

The *Original*

Le Sliceur.

pat. pend. © (TM) (R) (etc.)

(Manufacturer's note: All instructions are to be read with Strong Frrench Accent)

PRESENTEENG THEE NEW MODERRN METHODE TO SLASH YOUR DOUGH AND MAKE HANDSOME BREAD.

Preparatione:

safe fingeurs.

Insert one MINORA blade on the end of your SLICEUR, weethout Sliceung your fingeurs.

Operatione:

Slash the dough at an angle, from one side to other, 1 inch from base. Praktees!

Maintenance: No Aqua!!!

I read on, amazed and amused. Small hand-drawn cartoons accompanied the instructions and I was completely taken in. (See illustration on p. ?) When it finally dawned on me that Niël had in fact made the remarkable little tool himself, I nearly hugged him to death. He had even included a personalised "H" on the rubber handle of "La Sliceur". To top it all, this little wonder works like a dream. I have used it ever since. In the same plastic box I keep a long darning needle for testing whether the bread is done.

May there be a brilliant inventor in every baker's life!

Once we started baking in the larger wood-fired oven and began to supply the Saturday morning market, my output grew dramatically. This meant working with much larger quantities of dough, often more than ten kilograms at a time. I discovered quite a few techniques to cut down on the kneading, but even so, handling all that heavy dough started to get the better of me. Chronic pain and stiff shoulders seemed to be my lot. But I understood that my body was warning me, and over the years I have learnt to heed her signals. If I wanted to be a baker, I would have to get a proper kneading machine.

I left for Cape Town with a few addresses in my pocket. First I looked at places that sell second-hand baking equipment but soon discovered that decent mixers are hard to find. I also wanted to avoid landing up with someone else's discarded problem. Prices varied tremendously. At last one dealer took me to the heart of the industrial area near Paardeneiland, and that is where I found what I needed. Mixers with attitude. I wanted to buy the smallest model industrial mixer, but soon realised that even these would be too small to handle my large quantities of dough. Finally I spotted her: a twenty litre planetary mixer: a sturdy, compact machine with a central mixing arm and an adequate steel mixing bowl. Made in China. The price was shocking, but I had to admit she was the one I wanted. I also bought a second-hand steel trolley as a base.

Fortunately Mrs Armstrong fitted into my car's boot, and today she has pride of place on Poena's stoep, neatly dressed in a shweshe overcoat that Lies sewed for her. At first I was a bit envious of Mrs A. Would she rob me of the pleasure of touching the dough? But it was soon clear that we would each have a role to play. Once she has done her part to mix the flour and water into a homogenous mass, I take over. I fold the dough by hand until it feels ready. And after the first fermentation there is further work for my hands, in the weighing and shaping of the dough.

Granted, my assistant was expensive, but without her I would never have been able to cope.

✦

If you are privileged to bake in a wood-fired oven, you will need a few special tools. Firstly you will need a long spatula with which to move the dough into and out of the hot oven. This is known as a peel. It is a flat wooden paddle attached to a long handle. My cousin Carin has made us a few beautiful ones from thin plywood. The exact shape and size required quite a bit of experimentation. The edges need to be thin and smooth enough to slip under a cooked loaf without damaging the crust. Peels are also used to move loaves around inside the oven to ensure that they bake evenly. Kitchen suppliers may stock metal peels typically used for pizza ovens.

Lies uses two specialised tools for managing the fire. The first is a long copper pipe, flattened at the one end, for moving coals and wood around in the oven. The other is a metal scraper for raking out the ashes and coals from the oven at the end of the bake. See the illustration on p for the model which was specially made for us by our local ironmonger. Be warned that the scraper has to be as light as possible, to prevent unnecessary strain on the stoker's back and shoulders.

An old-fashioned shovel is useful for scooping up the ashes before dumping them in a metal bin, or in our case, an ash hole under the oven. Wood ash is excellent for the compost heap.

Then one also needs a mop to clean the floor of the oven before the bread goes in. Niël fabricated our first mop by tying an old shirt to an apricot twig. The piece of cloth is first dunked into a bucket of water, wrung our lightly and then swept over the sizzling hot oven floor from back to front. Needless to say, light-weight cotton does not last long. Our second mop was my once favourite cotton nightdress from Spain. The lacework was soon gone but it worked well, at least for a while. In time we had to move beyond these primitive measures and started looking for a proper mop. Modern mops mostly have plastic fittings and cannot be used in a hot oven. One day at Van Tonder's – where else? – we found the ideal mop: cotton fibres attached to the wooden handle with a wire fitting.

Of course almost all of this equipment can be bought in expensive shops. But my patient collection of just the right bits and pieces has given me a sense of tremendous pleasure. It confirms my feeling that I belong to an ancient tradition of simple hunters and gatherers.

6

Basic Bread-Making: Ingredients and
Techniques

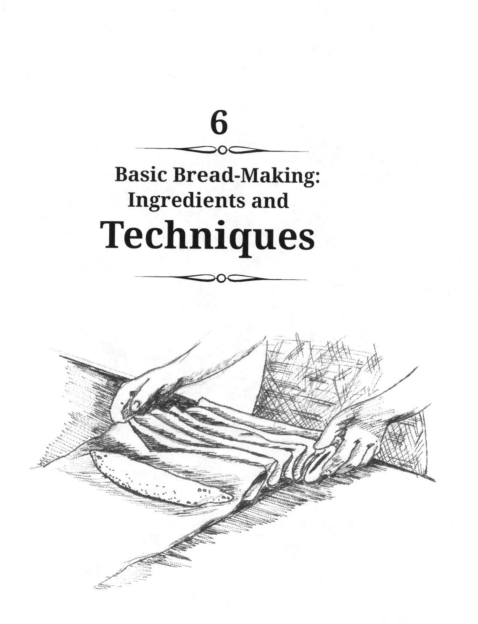

First the good news. The requirements for producing the most delicious bread are really very few – all you need is flour, water, yeast and salt, and an oven or a fire. The bad news for modern folks is that you do need time and patience. With a little planning, however, it is possible to devise a baking schedule that will suit almost any personal lifestyle.

In this chapter I want to tell you all I've learnt about the ingredients and the basic technique of bread-making.

Ingredients

Flour

The white bread flour available in any supermarket is perfectly suitable for home baking, but I prefer to experiment with flour produced by local millers in my area, such as the stone-ground flour from Eureka Mills near Heidelberg. White bread flour can be used together with brown and whole wheat flour and wheat germ. For my multigrain loaf (*see recipe in Chapter 9, p ?*) I use crushed whole wheat and crushed rye that is soaked overnight in order to render it more easily digestible.

What about gluten, the latest topic of food writers? Wheat contains more gluten that any other cereal. Gluten consists of several proteins which form a network of cells when it comes into contact with water. It has an important role in the development of dough because of a quality known as visco elasticity. This elasticity enables the baker to create endless shapes from dough. When the dough is fully developed the gluten network keeps air bubbles trapped in the dough.

Rye flour contains no gluten, but has different proteins, namely gliadine and gluteline. It also contains pentosan, the gluey substance that makes rye dough so difficult to handle because it tends to stick to everything. The best advice is to handle it as lightly and as little as possible and to avoid over-proofing. Rye is mainly grown in cold climates and is not so readily available in local shops. There is one roller mill in Citrusdal that mills rye on a big scale.

Water

Fermentation starts as soon as flour is mixed with water. Use the cleanest water you have; tap water is usually good enough.

Yeast

A yeast cell is a living organism; a single fungus cell. Yeast cells exist freely in nature, but some species are cultured for specific uses. Commercial bread yeast, *saccharomyces cervisiae,* was developed from the yeast used for beer brewing. The metabolic processes of yeast cells assist with the rising of bread dough. The yeast cells feed on the carbohydrates (complex sugars) in the flour, and the end products are carbon dioxide – the gas which causes the bread to rise – and alcohol. The conversion of carbohydrate takes place under the influence of the enzymes amylase and diastase, and this process is known as fermentation. In the ideal environment, and given sufficient time, yeast cells will continue to multiply until their waste products – mainly alcohol and acetic acid – start poisoning them, or until their food supply runs out. It takes a few hours for the enzymes to do their job and therefore a slow fermentation always yields a better loaf of bread. That explains why bread that was grown from a starter or fore-dough always tastes so good.

Dough will rise at any temperature between about 4 – 40 degrees Celsius. The slower the fermentation, the more acid the taste. If the temperature is too high, the bread will ferment fast and may have an unpleasant aftertaste.

The most important principle is to use the bare minimum of yeast to cause the bread to rise. You will notice that the recipes in this book require far less yeast than most commonly available recipes. Excessive yeast does work much more quickly, but it digests the carbohydrates too fast and tends to leave an after-taste of alcohol. Too much yeast and accelerated fermentation are to blame for the poor quality of most mass-produced bread.

Different types of commercial yeasts are available, but recipes in this book simply require the dried instant yeast which is sold in 10 gram packets.

See Chapter 8, p 125 for instructions on how to make your own wild yeast for sourdough bread.

Salt

Apart from enhancing the flavour of bread, salt has another important function. It retards fermentation, giving the dough sufficient time to develop taste and texture. Ordinary table salt works perfectly.

Seeds

Sunflower and sesame seeds can be dry roasted (without oil) in a skillet before adding them to a flour mixture. I prefer to add linseed to the starter dough to soften the seeds for better digestion.

Oil

Olive oil can be added to the dough of flatbreads, such as ciabatta or pita breads. The oil gives taste and softens the texture of dough.

Olive oil or herb oils can also be dribbled over the dough before baking, for flavour and colour.

Sugar

Contrary to popular belief, bread dough does not require sugar for fermentation. I add sugar only to sweet doughs, for instance raisin bread or certain types of kitkes.

Equipment

Your kitchen is probably fully equipped with basics such as an oven, mixing bowls, wooden spoons, cooling racks and bread tins. So here I only mention a few further items that could add pleasure and ease to your baking adventures.

I highly recommend a digital scale. Weighing ingredients is far more accurate than working with cup measures. My scoop of flour may differ quite a bit from your scoop of flour. A scale without a bowl works best. You place your mixing bowl directly on the scale, set the dial to "0" and add the right amount of water. Set the dial back to "0", then add the correct amount of flour. A useful tip: the volume of water equals its weight; thus one hundred millilitres of water equals one hundred grams of water.

A dough scraper is one of the handiest tools you can buy for a few rand. It is a rectangular piece of metal with a sharp cutting edge attached to a plastic or wooden handle. This little miracle helper helps you to scrape dough from your counter and to get the last bits of sticky dough from your mixing bowl. You could even scrape excess dough from your hands (but beware the sharp edge). The versatile scraper can also be used for lifting and moving slack dough and for cutting and dividing dough. Dough scrapers are sold by kitchen suppliers, but if you can't find one you could get a paint scraper from your hardware store.

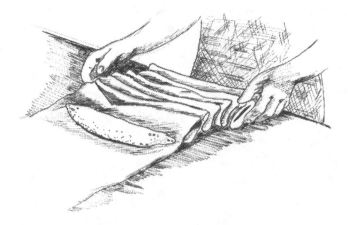

Dough cloths or couches *are indispensable.*

Couche means a layer or a diaper in French. These heavy linen cloths serve to support dough once it is shaped and needs to rise for the second time. They are particularly useful for supporting baguettes or ciabattas. Folds in the cloth support the sides of the dough, enabling it to expand upwards rather than sideways. The width of the rectangular cloth should be a little more than the length of your loaves and one to two meters long.

To arrange the couche, place the cloth on a large baking sheet or a tray. This will allow you to move the loaves around. Make a few pleats down the length of the cloth to form little tunnels for holding and separating the baguettes. (See illustration on this page.) Dust the cloth generously with flour to prevent the dough from sticking. With some practice the fully proofed loaves can be flipped from the pleat onto the baking tray without distorting its shape. You could easily make your own couches. Lies and I have stitched together a few layers of an old flannel sheet, old table cloths and kitchen towels. After use, the couches are hung out to dry in the sun and given a good shake before I fold and store them for the next bake. The remaining flour residue gives the cloth more substance and the remaining yeast cells add to the rich taste of your next batch.

For round loaves or floor breads, which are freestanding breads, you will need moulds. Because these loaves are not baked in tins but on a baking sheet or baking tile, they need the support of a mould while they are rising, so that they will rise upwards. The French use bannetons, special basket moulds made from willow and bamboo. You could improvise by using a plastic colander, or any round bowl or basket with sides that don't flare out too widely.

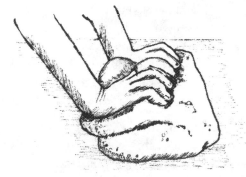

Techniques

Mixing and kneading the dough

There are many bread machines on the market these days, and of course there's nothing to stop you from mixing bread in your food processor, using the dough hook. But I strongly suspect that the real magic of bread-making is in touching the dough with your own hands. It is the physical contact that makes so many people fall in love with bread-making.

The word "knead" describes the way that hands and knuckles work a piece of clay or dough to refine its texture. According to my Oxford dictionary, to knead is "to press and stretch dough or to massage muscles".

Some people feel intimidated by sticky dough, but a few basic techniques will soon help you to adjust and enjoy the texture.

Weigh the ingredients into your mixing bowl. It doesn't matter much whether you start with water or flour, but try to keep back a little of the water. It is easier to add more water later if the dough is too dry, than it is to add more flour to wet dough.

Stir the ingredients well with a wooden spoon. Now use one of your hands to mix in the remaining bits of dry flour until you have a very rough mixture.

Cover the bowl with a cloth or slip it into a large plastic bag for 15 – 20 minutes. The resting period, or autolyse, first discovered by Professor Raymond Calvel, a famous French baker, allows the flour to absorb the water. You may feel tempted to regard it as a waste of time, but this simple step will cut down dramatically on the amount of time required later for kneading the dough.

Now turn the dough out onto your work surface. Do not be tempted to add extra flour at this stage; simply add the salt and the yeast. Salt retards the action of yeast, so avoid pouring them on top of each other. Put the salt and the yeast on opposite sides of the dough.

The dough should be much easier to handle after the resting period. Using both hands, pick up the edge of the dough furthest from you and fold it towards you, sealing the seam with the fleshy parts of your hand palms. Rotate the dough through 90 degrees, i.e. one quarter of the way. The dough scraper may be used to help with this. Again, lift the furthest edge of the dough, stretch it, fold it towards you and seal the seam. Repeat these lifting, stretching, folding and sealing motions rhythmically while you keep on rotating the dough. You will soon feel how the texture changes under your fingers – from a lumpy, sticky mass to a smooth, supple and uniform substance. After five or ten minutes the dough begins to feel warm, smooth and alive – hence the well-known comparison to a baby's bottom.

If you handle large quantities of dough, you need to work intelligently in order to prevent strain to your shoulders and arms. Fortunately my experience with t'ai chi has taught me how to maximise my energy. You need to be grounded first: place your feet shoulder-width apart, the right foot about half a step in front of the left. As your breathe in, lift the dough; then during your out breath, lean forward using your body weight to press down on the dough. You will note how much easier it is to use your whole body to rock forwards and backwards, instead of using only your arms and shoulders. If you become aware of tension in your jaw, neck or shoulders, make a conscious effort to relax all tightness. Soon you will transform kneading into a dance, or even a meditation, and you will be more present to everything that happens in and around you.

The gluten windowpane test

With experience you will soon learn to know when dough is fully kneaded, but in the beginning you can use a simple test. Pinch off an almond-sized ball of dough and carefully stretch it out between your fingers. If you can stretch it thinly to form a smooth, even, translucent sheet without tearing it, the gluten is well developed. If it forms a lumpy sheet which tears easily, it is barely developed and needs more kneading.

Turning and folding the dough

Another useful method for developing the best dough is to turn and fold it a few times during the first hour of fermentation. Set your timer for twenty minutes after you have finished kneading the dough. When it is time, transfer the dough back to your working surface and use your fingers and the palms of your hands to flatten it out into a rectangle. Pick up the left edge and fold it towards the middle of the rectangle. Repeat the same lifting and folding action with the remaining three edges. Return the tightly shaped bundle of dough to the bowl, seam-side down, and cover with plastic or a cloth. Repeat the turning and folding procedure twice more at twenty minute intervals.

Fermentation: The first rise

The quality of your bread will largely be determined during this dramatic stage, when the dough transforms from a lifeless lump to a living organism. The process can take anything from one to three hours, depending on the type of bread and the temperature.

Commercial bakeries manipulate fermentation time by regulating the temperature in special proofing boxes. This enables them to plan their baking schedules. Home bakers can use similar principles to plan their baking. By leaving dough in your fridge overnight you can retard fermentation. Ascetic acid, which gives a characteristic sour tang to the bread, develops during slower fermentation. At higher temperatures the dough will ferment much more quickly and will produce a nasty aftertaste. Dough that has spent time in the fridge needs to be left out for an hour or so to return to room temperature.

How do we know when dough is fully developed? It will more or less double in volume because it is filled with carbon dioxide. Here is a simple test: Dip your fingertip in flour and gently poke a hollow in the dough. If the dent bounces back quickly, the dough is not yet ready; if the dent fills out slowly, the dough is well fermented; if, however, the dent remains hollow, your dough is probably over-fermented and this means trouble. Over-fermented dough will not have the necessary resilience to retain its structure during shaping or to rise again later. Under-fermentation is definitely preferable to over-fermentation!

Degassing or punching down

It is not absolutely necessary to knead the dough a second time, but it should certainly be degassed after the first fermentation. This gets rid of excessive carbon dioxide trapped in the gluten network and allows the gluten to relax. It also helps to redistribute the sugars and make them available to feed the yeast during the second rise.

Different types of dough require different handling. Wet doughs, such as ciabatta for instance, call for gentle handling. Simply turning out the dough on your work surface should be sufficient to get rid of excess gases. Firm doughs can be folded again, as explained previously under "Turning and folding". Remember always to turn the dough parcel over seam-side under, and to cover it again.

Dividing the dough

If you have enough dough for two or more loaves, this is the time to cut it up with your dough scraper or a sharp knife. Practiced bakers soon develop the knack of dividing the mass accurately. It is best not to make too many cuts, as these disturb the internal structure of the dough. Dough should never be torn or ripped.

> ## *Note:
> Dough should never be torn or ripped.

Rounding and resting

Each piece of dough should now be rounded to create a taut, dry outer skin which will keep the bubbles intact. The elasticity of the outer skin enables us to form dough into different shapes. A simple way to round dough is to turn the dough skin-side up on the counter and to tuck in loose ends by cupping your hands around the ball. Form a tight seam at the bottom of the ball by pinching the loose ends together. You will feel the skin stretching and growing tauter as you create more surface tension.

Place the rounded balls of dough seam-side down on a lightly floured surface. Cover with plastic to prevent drying, and rest the dough for 15 to 20 minutes. This will allow the air to spread evenly and the gluten to relax, creating a more supple dough for shaping during the next phase.

Shaping the loaves

Every recipe in this book has specific guidelines for shaping loaves. As mentioned before, you will need special moulds such as baskets or dough cloths to support the dough as it rises into its required shape during the second and rising. It will take quite a bit of practice to shape a perfect baguette, so be patient with yourself!

Proofing – the second rise

During this stage the well covered dough grows into its final rise in preparation for baking. The ideal temperature for proofing is 21 degrees Celsius. Each recipe will suggest an ideal proofing time, but be aware that the micro-climate of your kitchen, the type of dough, and even the type of flour you've used, will make your dough unique. It is useful to test the dough again for readiness by using the same pressure test described during the first rise. As a general guide, dough is fully proofed when it looks well risen but retains sufficient elasticity for the final rise in the oven.

Scoring or cutting the dough

As soon as the loaves are fully proofed and ready to be baked, you can score the tops. These cuts are not simply decorative; they also release some of the trapped gases and allow the dough to expand during the final oven rise (see the section below on baking). A loaf that is not scored tends to burst, usually in unattractive places such as the side or the bottom.

The ideal blade should be thin and sharp to avoid stretching or indenting the tightly stretched skin of the dough. (See p 78 for a description of the improvised cutting tool made by my friend Niël.) An old fashioned shaving blade works well. The blade is held at a 45 degree angle to the surface of the dough. The cuts should never be too close to the edges of the loaf. Start about three centimetres from one edge and end three centimetres from the opposite edge. Your aim is to make a thin, nearly horizontal incision, never deeper than about one and a half centimetres. The sharp blade should slip lightly through the dough, without any pressure.

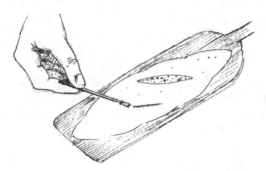

Traditionally each type of loaf is cut in a characteristic manner. Baguettes are scored with a few perpendicular cuts that slant down the length of the loaf. Round loaves look beautiful with a large C or an X. Smaller rolls can be snipped with a pair of scissors. These little points result in a lovely crunchy crust. The crust of a well scored loaf opens like a flower or a smile in the oven. Hence the French term, *"la grigne"*!

Baking the bread

The breads in this book are mainly hearth breads, which means that they are baked on top of a baking tin or oven rack, and not in loaf tins. Take care to leave enough space around each loaf or bread roll for air to circulate freely around the entire surface. This will ensure a crisp crust. If individual loaves or rolls are too close to each other, they tend to rise sideways instead of vertically.

Here are a few tips on how to achieve the benefits of hearth baking in your own oven.
Peel the loaves directly onto a preheated baking tin or a baking stone. A thick rectangular stone will retain its heat more effectively

than a sheet pan. Alternatively you could ask the nearest potter for an unglazed quarry tile. The tile should be in place while you preheat your oven.

Another way of emulating a professional bread oven is to introduce steam into the oven during the first half of the bake. As soon as you close the oven door, the dough is surrounded by hot air. Just imagine the yeast taking one last gulp of air to achieve the final rise, also known as oven spring. Steam in the oven delays the hardening of the outer crust, allowing the dough to expand.

The most effective way to introduce steam is to place a heavy steam pan on the lowest shelf of the oven. Just before putting the dough in the oven, pour one cup of boiling water into the steam pan. The oven will immediately fill with steam. Slide the loaves into the oven and close the door.

Many bakers tend to under-bake their bread, either because their ovens are not hot enough or because they take the bread from the oven too soon. Remember that it is the caramelisation of the crust that gives hearth bread its depth of taste. For most types of bread, preheat your oven to its maximum 230 degrees Celsius. After 10 or 15 minutes of baking, turn down the heat. Check your bread half-way through the bake and turn the loaves to ensure even baking.

Cooling the loaves

Now for the most difficult part – to wait patiently until the bread is cool enough to cut! Like most children I never believed my mother when she cautioned us against stomach cramps when we insisted on eating bread hot from the oven. But yes, it is true – the bread continues cooking after it is taken from the oven. While cooling, the crumb, or inside of the bread, continues to evaporate moisture and the starches continue to settle. If cut too soon, the loaf will be soggy and the taste will not be fully developed.

Cool loaves at room temperature on a cooling rack to promote free circulation of air.

Storing bread

If there is still some bread left after baking day, place it in an airtight plastic bag, or wrap it in a clean linen or cotton cloth until the following day or two. If you plan to store bread for longer periods, it is best sealed in plastic and frozen. I prefer to slice whole wheat loaves before freezing them, and to remove as much as I need every day.

A tip for refreshing stale bread is to spray the crust with water and to place the bread in a hot oven (200 degrees Celsius) for about 10 minutes.

7

The Classic
Baguette
– Air Wrapped In Dough

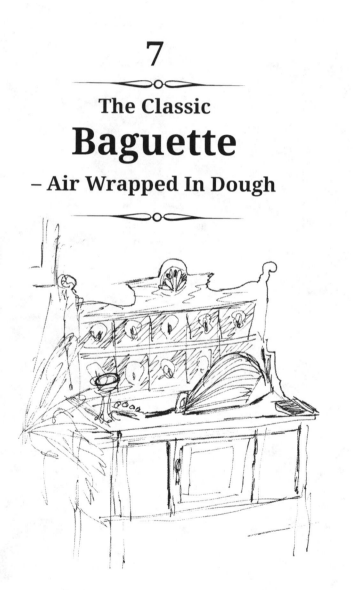

These iconic long loaves first appeared on the streets of Paris around the nineteen twenties. Today, I'm told, an authentic baguette is harder to come by in France than hen's teeth. Similarly, the "French bread" commonly available in our own supermarkets is often a sad lumpy version of the real thing. Why is this? Because real baguette dough requires a complex fermentation process, and yes, you're right – this requires planning and time!

The good news, however, is that the technique is fairly easy and with some care, you can make perfect baguettes at home. Because the baguette's large surface area exists almost entirely of crust, the challenge is to achieve a crisp crust while maintaining a soft inner crumb. For this, steam will come to your rescue. (See "Baking the Bread" in Chapter 6.)

It does require skill to shape a baguette. The goal is to get the outer skin of the dough tautly stretched around the air-filled inner dough. Imagine air wrapped in dough. This will take practice, but with time you will learn how to handle the dough firmly yet with just the right measure of gentleness. The proverbial iron fist in the velvet glove! But relax; even if your first baguettes turn out somewhat skew, they will nevertheless taste heavenly.

In 2008 Anis Bouabsa, a Parisian baker, won the prize for the best baguettes in the annual Grand Prix de la Baguette de Tredition Francaise de la Ville de Paris. Instead of beginning with the traditional starter dough, Bouabsa opted for just one long cold fermentation. This is good news for the home baker, as it reduces the preparation time by half and involves much less hands-on work. Although in the Afrikaans version of this book (Hester se Brood, 2009) I still recommended the use of a starter dough, I have here adopted Bouabsa's approach, and have adapted his prize-winning recipe for local flour. Have fun!

Recipe notes

> Timing: You will need at least 24 hours to make this bread. After the dough is mixed it will need to be left in the fridge for 21 to 48 hours. Thereafter it will be divided into three or four portions and rested for an hour at room temperature. When the loaves have been shaped, the dough will need to proof for a further one to one and a half hours before baking can commence. The actual baking time will be about 20 minutes.

> Suggested schedule: Mix the dough before going to bed; take it out of the fridge at about 4.30 the next afternoon; shape and proof the baguettes; bake them; and serve them for dinner.

> The following recipe yields four small baguettes or three larger ones.

> For a quick recap, see the section on Techniques in Chapter 6.

Dough

520 g (4 cups) white bread flour

350 g/ml water

¼ teaspoon instant yeast

10 g salt

Mix the flour and water in a bowl to form a rough dough. Cover bowl with plastic and autolyse for 20 minutes.

Add yeast and salt and mix into the dough by stretching and folding the dough for 5 to 10 minutes.

Turn and fold the dough three more times at twenty minute intervals during the next hour. The dough should become smooth, slightly sticky, but easy to handle.

Place the dough in a lightly oiled bowl cover tightly and refrigerate for 21 to 48 hours.

Remove the dough from the fridge and divide into 3 or 4 balls. Pre-shape the dough by forming each ball into an oval (rugby ball) shape. Place the ovals on lightly floured surface and cover with plastic.

Allow the dough to rest for one hour at room temperature.

While the dough rests, prepare a well floured dough cloth that will support your swelling baguettes between deep concertina pleats. (See the section on Couches under "Equipment" in Chapter 6.) Place the dough cloth on a baking sheet or tray, to allow you to move around your kitchen.

Prepare a baking sheet. The length of your sheet will determine the length of your shaped baguettes. Unfortunately you will be limited by the size of your oven.

Early during baking day she is in her own little world – flies, goggas and so on. Happy in her world because she knows love, warmth and softness.

23 December 2004

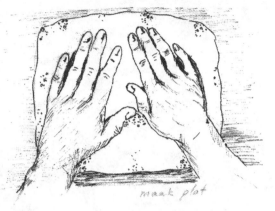

Shaping the baguette

This is one of the most complex shapes to master, so be patient. Actually it sounds more difficult than it really is. Basically it consists of a series of three folds, aimed at stretching the outer skin of the dough tautly over the inside, thereby increasing surface tension. A taut skin will stretch to accommodate an even rise.

Here's how to do it: Take one of the rested pieces of dough and place it on a lightly floured working surface, skin side down. Gently flatten the dough with your palm into a rough rectangle, with one of its long sides towards you.

First fold: Fold the long side closest to you upwards, just past the middle of the rectangle. Press down on the open seam to seal it.

Second fold: Lift the other long side of the rectangle and fold it downwards towards you. Press down on the seam to seal it. You should now have a rectangle that looks like a folded business letter. In fact, the dough is beginning to take on the cylindrical shape of a baguette.

Third fold: Make a trough along the centre seam with the side of your hand. Note how this action lengthens the cylinder even further. Now fold the top side of the cylinder all the way down towards you and seal it to the edge closest to you, thus folding the sausage in half lengthways. Start the sealing action in the middle of the seam and work outwards. Press down firmly on your work surface to ensure a secure seam that will keep the bubbles sealed inside the roll.

> Note: If your dough sausage still feels too limp after all these folds, all is not lost. Simply repeat the third fold.

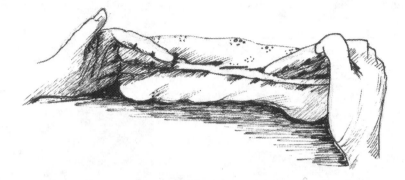

Lengthening and narrowing the cylinder: Place the sausage, seam-side down, on a clean, very lightly floured surface. Ideally the dough needs to grip the surface without slipping. With your palms facing downwards, place your one hand over the other over the centre of the roll. The heel of your hand and your fingertips should touch the work surface, while your palm rests firmly on the dough. Move your hands back and forth, from fingertips to heel, in a rolling motion to narrow the cylinder from the centre outwards. As the roll begins to narrow, start moving your hands in opposite directions towards the thicker ends while you continue the rolling motion.

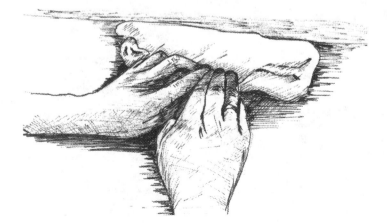

The idea is not to stretch the dough, but rather to move your hands outwards in response to the narrowing of the dough. When you reach the ends of the cylinder, apply a bit more downward rolling pressure to make the points at each end. In the end the cylinder should be about 4 centimetres shorter than your baking tin.

Proofing

Place each baguette in a pleat of the well-floured dough cloth. Slip the entire couche into a large plastic bag for the final rise of 60 to 90 minutes, depending on the temperature in your kitchen.

Baking

Pre-heat your oven to 230 degrees Celsius. Place an empty steam pan in the bottom of the oven, and a baking stone or baking sheet on the rack ready to receive the loaves.

When the dough is fully proofed, lift two baguettes onto your pre-heated baking stone or sheet. Score each loaf by making three angled cuts across the length of the loaf.

Place the baguettes in the oven. Pour one cup of boiling water in the steam pan and close the oven door. Bake for 15 to 20 minutes, or until the "ears" of the cuts are dark brown and the breads are a deep golden brown.

Cool the loaves on a cooling rack for at least 40 minutes before tucking in.

8

Sourdough:
The Mother Of All
Bread

How to use and maintain a sourdough mother

Remove inactive mother from fridge. Feed with flour and water

8 hours later mother is active and ready for use

Divide mother into two parts.

Add active mother to starter dough

Save one part of mother for later use

About 4 hours later Add starter dough to dough

Please note:

Take good care of your mother to keep her alive and bubbly.

Share her with friends and fellow bread lovers.

Take her from the fridge in time for your baking cycle.

Thank her for working on your behalf while you rest.

Bread!

On no! What is this? I was very disappointed when I took my Karoo loaves from the oven last Friday. Instead of the anticipated jovial smiles on their upper crusts the loaves all had lopsided bulges, like early pregnancies. Instead of the usual earthy russet glow, they were a dull brown. The dough had looked perfectly normal and had been fairly easy to shape. Something had definitely gone wrong somewhere. I could think of two possible causes. The dough had either been over-proofed, or the sourdough mother had not been lively enough. Perhaps the time had come to give the wild yeast mother a good wash.

But first I need to tell you more about the mysterious world of sourdough starters, or mothers.

What is the secret of a perfect loaf of bread? The quality of the fermentation process. The secret is to use just enough yeast to cause the dough to rise and unlock the full flavour from the wheat. At the start of this book I referred to Nancy Silverton's passion for sourdough and her low opinion of short cuts such as the use of commercial yeast. If you longed to sink your teeth into that magical marriage between crust and crumb, you had to be prepared to start from scratch, and this meant making your own sourdough culture. Or, put differently, to patiently set the trap for the wild yeast spores which surround us.

At the time, nothing could curb my enthusiasm. I was determined to follow Nancy every step of the way. But you need patience for her method – a full fourteen days for nurturing your own sourdough culture. And let me tell you, this little mother looks pretty grim at first: a grey, smelly mixture. You start with a mixture of water, flour and a bunch of grapes on the stem. Eventually you strain the mixture to remove the grapes and start with a daily feed of flour and water. In time you discard the excess mixture, to avoid ending up with buckets full of hungry mother which requires flour three times a day.

By the end of this lengthy story, and given my dedication, I could hardly wait to start baking. Nancy's meticulous step by step instructions took me by surprise. Each baking project required at least two days of work. Her motto was clear: It is not hard to make perfect bread; all it requires is time! I did my best to follow her instructions, but alas – the results were not great. My notes at the time tell a sad tale: small holes, slightly sour flavour, sticky crumb. Even I had to admit my disappointment, especially after all that diligence.

Three years later, I met another bread guru, Peter Reinhart, who inspired me once again to build a sourdough culture. His user-friendly process takes only five days. And the result looked more promising – a thick creamy mama which responded by blowing bubbles when stirred with a wooden spoon. With her, you were soon ready to make your first sourdough loaf! At the end of this chapter I explain how to grow a sourdough starter in five days.

There is further good news: you don't need to start from scratch for every batch of bread. Simply save about one cup of your starter to use as a base for your next batch. Give the mother a permanent home in your fridge. It all depends on how often you bake. For instance, I have a weekly baking cycle. Every Wednesday night I remove the mother from my fridge and feed her flour and water, thus doubling the volume and re-activating the yeast. Within eight hours (depending on the temperature) she rises vigorously and the next morning she is ready to be used in my starter dough.

The sketch on p illustrates and summarises the life cycle of a sourdough mother.

Have you heard of the legendary San Francisco sourdough bread? This bread is produced with a sourdough mother that is reputedly centuries old. The fact is that all sourdough cultures are colonised by yeast cells and bacteria which occur freely in our natural environment.

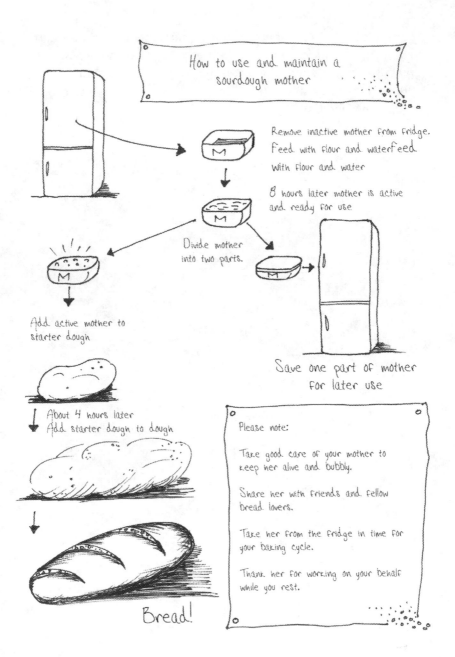

How to use and maintain a sourdough mother

Remove inactive mother from fridge. Feed with flour and waterfeed with flour and water

8 hours later mother is active and ready for use

Divide mother into two parts.

Add active mother to starter dough

Save one part of mother for later use

About 4 hours later Add starter dough to dough

Bread!

Please note:

Take good care of your mother to keep her alive and bubbly.

Share her with friends and fellow bread lovers.

Take her from the fridge in time for your baking cycle.

Thank her for working on your behalf while you rest.

Tracing the sourdough tradition of our grandmothers

"Do you use potatoes?" they all ask me at the market. "No," I say. "I know that our grannies used a potato culture to raise their dough, but I use ordinary wheat flour and water to maintain my culture. Yes Madam, just like a yoghurt plant that people pass on to their friends."

Silence. The client gets a faraway gaze and I know she is no longer with me. She is in her granny's kitchen in front of the black Dover. She smells the loaves puffing in the loaf tins. She hears Ouma's warning, "You can't have any now. It must cool first!"

All the questions made me curious about potato yeast. There are many stories. Some insist that you use boiled potatoes plus the water in which they were cooked. Well, one day Kitty, my neighbour, brought me one of her sister's books, *Boerekos: Tradisionele Suid-Afrikaanse Resepte,* by Dine van Zyl. *Published in 1985 by Human & Rousseau*, this is a fairly modern book, with colour photographs and metric measurements. In the chapter that deals with baking, two recipes grabbed my attention. One was for a sweet sourdough bread (soet suurdeegbrood) that starts with potato yeast.

But first let me tell you about the other one: must rusks, or mosbolletjies.

The author grew up in Robertson and when I read how the village women always fetched must from her father's wine cellar, I sat up and took notice. The grape harvest in our valley was in full swing! So off I set with my plastic container and at our local cellar I asked for one litre of must for mosbolletjies. The young man took my container and disappeared behind the tall stainless steel vats of the modern cellar. After a few minutes I was back in my car.

I removed the plastic lid and took a peep at the bubbly, golden aromatic fluid. It tasted like grape juice but packed a hefty kick.

Dine van Zyl's mother's recipe must have filled many biscuit tins because it calls for four kilograms of flour to three cups of must. I adjusted the recipe and mixed one kilogram of flour. I added raisins and sultanas to the dough, which I mixed in the late afternoon. I covered the bowl and left it overnight. The next morning the dough had risen to the edge of the bowl. I followed Dine's advice: "Under no circumstances should you knead or deflate the dough." This, she promised, would be the secret of the "beautiful feathery texture" that distinguishes mosbeskuit from ordinary rusks. And was she right! The mosbolletjies were so good that we scoffed them all with butter before there was time to dry them in the oven.

Dine van Zyl's other recipe, the one for sweet sourdough bread, was handed down from Tannie Jossie Bouwer. She starts at two in the afternoon by mixing raw potato slices, boiling water, salt, sugar and whole meal. This step is known as insuur, or the souring in stage. The mixture is not stirred, but only covered and left in a warm place. The next morning it is time to sour over, by adding boiling water and one cup of flour to the initial mixture. It is covered again and will be ready for use after one hour. One is urged not to be in a hurry, but it is not clear what to watch for. I imagine that the mixture needs to show signs of live fermentation. Next, the potatoes are removed and the dough is mixed by adding flour, salt and lukewarm water. The dough is shaped, panned and brushed with melted butter "to prevent cracks".

During my search for the origins of potato fermentation, I discovered that potatoes have been used for this purpose for a very long time. Elizabeth David, my favourite food writer, describes a yeast recipe by Mrs Rundell published in 1806. She mixed cooked mashed potatoes with hops. Yeast mixes used by French settlers in Quebec also contained potatoes. In some instances potatoes were first boiled and mashed and then left to grow mouldy and dry. Just before use, the dried potatoes were soaked in a mixture of sugar and water.

The French used raisins or apples for starting a sourdough culture. But there is consensus among experts that a mixture of whole wheat and rye flour is the best medium for sourdough culture. This makes sense, seeing that the micro-flora on grains are already well adapted to dough and will produce flavours that are more natural to bread. Rye flour is ideal for starting a culture because its high mineral content promotes the growth of micro-organisms.

If you bake regularly, once or twice a week, you could hold back a portion of your dough to "seed" your following batch. This leftover, or "old" dough, could be kept in your fridge. Traditionally the seed was kept in a cloth flour bag. French bakers call this type of culture levain chef or pâte fermentée

Sourdough fermentation

In Chapter 6 I explained how commercial yeast assists fermentation. Let's now look at the mechanics of sourdough fermentation. Sourdough culture or mother contains natural wild yeast (usually Saccaramyces exiguus) which prefers an acid environment. However, the complex sour flavour is not created by the wild yeast, but by bacterial fermentation caused by lactobacilli and acetobacilli, which create lactic and acetic acids respectively. In the end, the complex flavour of a sourdough loaf is determined by the delicate balance of these two acids. An excess of acetic acid will produce a sharp vinegary flavour, while an excess of lactic acid will render the bread tasteless. Lactic acid develops relatively faster than ascetic acid. Bakers who favour a more sour taste tend to slow down fermentation by refrigerating the dough, thereby ensuring more time for ascetic acid to develop.

A note on terminology

> It is easy to become confused by all the different names given to the starter used in dough-making, especially when it comes to sourdough cultures. The Italians refer to la madre. The English talk of mother, leaven, or barm. Barm is a term borrowed from the beer industry. In Afrikaans I use the term suurdesem-moeder. In this book I refer to sourdough mother or sourdough starter for the culture.

> The following instructions for growing your own culture are based on Peter Reinharts recipe from The Bread Bakers Apprentice. Niël Jonker and I adapted it for our Passionate Bread-Making workshop in 2004.

> These measurements are less precise, so I include cup measurements.

Grow your own sourdough starter in five days

130 g (1 cup)

whole wheat flour or rye*

120 g/ml (¾ cup)

warm water

Day One

Mix the ingredients until they form a firm ball. Kneading is not required.

Put the dough in a clean cylindrical glass jar, and cover with cling-wrap.

Store the container in a warm place for 24 hours.

---

* The husks of whole meal flour and rye provide an ideal growth medium for micro-flora.

Day Two

At this stage the culture should contain small air bubbles and should give off a sharp smell. (If not, leave for another 12 to 24 hours until signs of fermentation are visible. A tablespoon of honey may also be added to the first day's ingredients, should fermentation have failed and the process need to be re-started.)

130 g (1 cup)

white bread flour

90g/ml (½ cup) warm water

Mix the second day's flour and water into the culture, following the same instructions as on Day One. With a strip of masking tape, mark the top level of the culture on the outside of the jar.

Cover the jar and store in a warm place for 24 hours.

130g (1 cup)
white bread flour
90g/ml (½ cup) warm water

Day Three

By now the culture should have doubled in size. If not, proceed regardless.

Discard half of the dough and mix the third day's ingredients into the remaining half, following the same instructions as on Day One.

Cover the jar, marking the dough level as before.

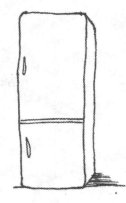

Day Four

The culture should definitely have doubled this time.

130g (1 cup) white bread flour

90g/ml (½ cup) warm water

Repeat the same process of discarding and feeding as on Day Three.

Cover the jar and mark the dough level.

The culture should again double in size, becoming spongy and soft. This may take between 4 to 24 hours.

520g (4 cups) white bread flour

360g/ml (2 cups) warm water

130 -160 g/ml (1 cup) culture

Day Five

Mix the fifth day's ingredients into a wet and sticky mixture. Discard the surplus culture or pass it on to a friend.

Cover and store in a clean jar in a warm place, after again marking the jar with tape.

The fermentation will now be more visible as the yeast creates gas and expands the cling wrap into a bubble. Release the gas each time this happens.

Store in the fridge overnight.

Congratulations, you have now grown your own sourdough starter and it is ready to be used! Try the recipe for multi-grain sourdough bread on p .

Please note that your starter will develop its full flavour only after the second or third bake. During this period the wild yeast and bacteria in your environment will gradually "populate" your starter.

Tips for using the sourdough starter

> Store your starter in a lidded container in the fridge.

> Always remove the starter from the fridge at least two hours prior to use.

> Ensure that you always retain about one cup of starter for the next bake.

> Dip spatulas, cups and other tools in water before you use them to work with the starter. This makes for a less sticky experience.

> Remember to feed the starter regularly, as explained below.

> After feeding, the starter can be stored in the fridge for up to a week before it needs another feeding. The starter performs best about twelve hours after a feed, when the yeast cells are at their most active and energised.

> Your starter may be stored in the fridge, in a dormant state, for up to three months without feeding. Following such a period, refresh the starter by washing it as follows: Put 1 cup starter into a large jar. Discard the rest. Fill the jar with warm water and stir well. Discard all except one cup of the fluid. Add one cup of flour and 3/4 cup warm water. Stir well, cover and ferment at room temperature until the yeast cells regain their activity.

Feeding the sourdough starter

Feeding your starter is not a precise science, but a useful guideline is to at least double the starter's volume each time. You could also triple or quadruple it. The bigger the feed, the less sour your bread will be, as a larger feed will dilute the yeast cells. Yeast cells multiply faster than bacteria, so even a diluted sourdough starter should perform well.

Here are two examples for feeding a sourdough starter.

To double the starter for a moderately sour bread, mix the following:

  130g or 160 ml (1 cup) sourdough starter

  90g/ml (½ cup) water

  65g (1/2 cup) white bread flour

For a less sour loaf, mix the following:

  130g or 160 ml (1 cup) sourdough starter

  270g/ ml (1½ cups) water

  200g (1½ cup) white bread flour

Now for a few favourite sourdough "mother tales" to end the chapter.

One of my best bread adventures was during a sourdough bread workshop for a group of potters who attended one of my neighbour, Paul de Jong's, pottery jamborees. At the end of the course I put up a list requesting the names of those who wanted to take home a sample of sourdough mother. Eleven people put their names on the list. I smiled, quietly thinking that only one or two of them would actually use the mother. Then my imagination ran wild and I began to picture possible scenarios back home. Pa gets home late on Sunday night with lots of stories about his pottery and baking weekend in McGregor. Two days later Ma discovers his kit bag and starts fishing out the dirty T-shirts. Everything is covered in dried clay and unmentionable dark stains. What did they get up to?! Honestly, they're just like a bunch of kids that go camping. In between all the messy bits she discovers a puffed up plastic bag, sealed with a red elastic band. It seems to be frothing with little bubbles. What Ma does next depends entirely on how curious, or brave she is. Most wives I know will carefully lift the bag between finger and thumb and chuck it in the bin. But one wife may hesitate, thinking that Pa may have brought back a special glaze that he will soon need. She puts it on the shelf where he keeps his other glaze powders …

Norman, one of the local potters, turned up to fetch his mother two days after the course. His eyes were twinkling mischievously under his grizzled crew cut. His wife Barbara, he tells me, had become really worried when she'd found a note he'd left himself on his desk: Fetch mother on Tuesday. Was Norman losing his memory? Both their mothers had been dead for years!

We had great fun thinking up all the possible misunderstandings the travelling mothers might spark off.

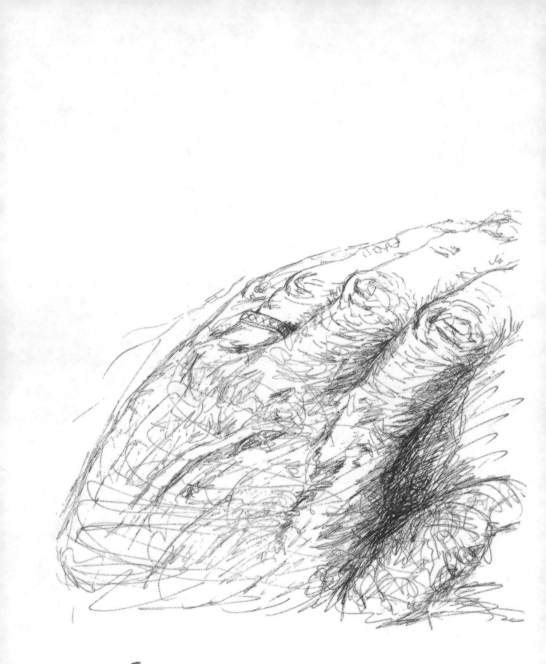

In the last rays of the winter sun.

9

Multigrain Sourdough
– The Bread of
Life

It was a great day when our Klein Karoo multigrain sourdough bread made its grand entrance at the Saturday morning market. This hearth loaf has a crisp crust textured like the rough stony ridges that surround our village, but when you bite into it the interior crumb is surprisingly soft and filled with irregular holes. The after-taste leaves a tangy sourdough flavour on the tongue.

Our adventure with multigrain sourdough began when Bread Brother Niël rocked up at Poena at 2 a.m. one Saturday morning in March. We had expected him for the night and had prepared a bed, but he did not turn up. Now here he was, just as we were rising to prepare for the day's bake. We were stumbling around the kitchen, eyes still heavy with sleep and partly blinded by the light. I was just beginning to sprinkle flour on my work surface, ready to pour out the prepared focaccia dough, when he appeared in the doorway.

"Yes! Yes! Can I light the fire?"

He was here to help us bake, he explained, but he also had a new trick he wanted to share – working with wet dough. "But don't worry," he assured us, "I promise not to disrupt you too much …"

I tried to keep a cool head as I divided and weighed the focaccia dough. One thing I had learnt a long time ago – with Niël around, anything could happen.

Niël had brought a sourdough starter in a plastic bucket. He fetched it from the passenger seat of his bakkie and carried it with a ceremonial show of respect into the kitchen. "Poolish!" he declared as he placed it on the table. He poured the starter into a large bowl, added flour, water and some soaked grains, and began to mix a wet and runny dough. I watched with a sceptical eye as he started stirring it rhythmically with one hand. After resting the mixture for a while, he stirred in the salt. Already there were signs of thickening. Then followed an astonishing stretch and fold routine which he repeated three times in the next hour. With one hand he steadied the bowl; with the other he lifted the floppy but surprisingly supple dough as much as half a meter into the air before lovingly laying it down again, neatly folded in half. The gluten developed before my eyes and after the third stretch and fold I could see how much firmer and more malleable the dough had become.

I had been baking for about two years by now, and this was my first introduction to working with really wet dough. I immediately called it Slap Sarel, or Sloppy Sam. Niël had been taught the technique in the United States by none other than Allan Scott, the famous oven builder and master baker from California.

Fired up by Niël's enthusiasm for this sloppy new dough, I began my own experiments in the weeks that followed, and now this has become the daily bread that we eat at our table. We love the firm chewy crust, the large uneven holes and the tell-tale sour tang. This is the type of bread that can be broken with a hearty soup or used to mop up a delicious sauce. On Saturday mornings I stand the loaves upright in a large basket marked "Klein Karoo", and in no time at all they are all sold out.

Recipe for multigrain sourdough

This recipe is based on Niël's Slap Sarel but I have made quite a few changes. I have added rye flour, seeds and soaked whole-wheat kernels. I suggest that you make this recipe your own by experimenting with different grains such as buckwheat, spelt, mealie meal, wheat germ and bran.

This bread lasts remarkably well. One of our clients who lives alone buys one loaf per week. She cuts it up, freezes it and takes out a few slices per day. It makes the best toast that you will ever have.

Recipe notes

The recipe requires an active sourdough mother that was last fed about eight hours before. (See Chapter 8 for information on how to feed and treat your sourdough mother.)

Suggested time schedule

Day One: 8 am. Feed your sourdough mother. 5 pm. Mix the two starters and leave them overnight.

Day Two: 8 am. Mix the dough. Midday Divide and shape the dough. 4 pm. Bake the bread.

> If you already have an active sourdough mother, you could produce this bread in one and a half days.

> The wet starter (poolish) needs at least four hours to ferment. Thereafter it can be kept in the fridge.

> Whole-wheat kernels and whole or cracked rye berries should be soaked while the starter dough develops. Soaking softens the grain and helps to activate enzymes and sugars which will enhance the breads flavour.

> Do experiment with different grains. For instance, replace 100 grams of white bread flour with the same quantity of oats or buckwheat.

> Regard this recipe as a lesson in handling wet dough by using the lift and fold technique. Do experiment with the amount of water. The amount depends largely on the types of grain. As you get more confident with handling wet dough, you could add more water.

> Allow at least three hours for the first rise.

> Thereafter the dough is divided, shaped and placed in containers for a proofing period of at least two to three hours.

> Baking takes about thirty-five to forty-five minutes.

> The recipe yields just over one kilogram of dough, enough for one large loaf plus a few rolls, or two smaller loaves.

Starter 1

130 g or 160 ml active sourdough mother

120 g/ml (3/4 cups) water

65 g (1/2 cup) with bread flour

65 g (1/2 cup) whole wheat flour

30 g (1/4 cup) rye flour

10 g (1 tablespoon) linseeds

Measure the sourdough mother and the water into your mixing bowl. Stir well. Add the three flours and the linseeds and mix with a wooden spoon. Cover the bowl by putting it into a large plastic bag. Allow to ferment at room temperature for 4 to 8 hours. During summer the starter can be placed in the fridge after 4 hours.

Starter 2

20 g (3 tablespoons) whole wheat kernels or crushed wheat

20 g (3 tablespoons) whole rye berries or crushed rye

80 g/ml (1/2 cup) boiling water

Combine all the ingredients in a lidded container. Leave overnight to soak.

Making the dough

Starter 1

Starter 2

200 – 250 g/ml water

300 g (2 ¼ cups) white bread flour

150 g (1 ¼ cup) whole wheat flour

20 g (2 tablespoons) sunflower seed

12 g (2 teaspoons) salt

Remove the first starter from the fridge one hour before making the dough. Add the soaked grains (second starter) plus about 170 g of the water and stir together. Add the two flours and stir well to mix. At this point you could add more of the water to ensure a runny texture. Cover the bowl and allow the dough to rest for 10 to 20 minutes.

First rise and folding of dough

From this point on, the dough will need three hours to ferment. The first hour is a busy time. Add the salt and the remaining 30 g of water to the dough. The dough should be very sticky and wet; too wet for ordinary kneading, hence the need to lift and fold it in order to develop the gluten.

Place a jug with water next to the mixing bowl. Dip your working hand and forearm into the water jug every now and then before touching the dough. This will keep the dough from sticking too much. Use your other hand to hold and turn the bowl. Try to keep this hand free of dough in case you need to answer the telephone!

With your working hand, scoop up the runny dough, lift it as high as you can above the bowl, then fold it back over the remaining dough. Let the fold fall towards you, thus from twelve o'clock downwards towards six o'clock. Turn the bowl through 90 degrees after each fold.

Continue this procedure for about 10 minutes. See Chapter 6 for a full description of the lift and turn procedure. The dough should steadily start firming up, becoming more elastic and easier to handle.

> Cover the bowl to rest for 10 minutes.

> Repeat the lift and fold procedure.

> This 20-minute cycle (10 minutes of folding followed by 10 minutes of rest) should be repeated three times in the course of the first hour. There after the dough should rest for a further two hours.

Dividing, shaping and proofing the dough

Dust your working surface with flour and tip out the dough. The outer skin should be firm while the interior should still be moist and alive with gas, most of which will escape as you gently handle the dough.

Divide the dough by cutting it into the number of loaves or rolls that you want. Gently shape each piece into a ball shape. Round the dough by placing it skin side up on your counter. Pinch the cut ends tightly together to form a seam. Lightly cover the dough pieces and rest them on the counter for 15 to 20 minutes.

Prepare baskets or other bread-form containers of choice for holding the dough in shape while proofing. Line each basket with a well-floured bread cloth. (See Chapter 6 for information on couches.) If you prefer traditional pan loaves, prepare one large or two smaller bread tins by spraying them with a baking spray or oiling them.

Shaping a round loaf or boulle

Using your dough scraper, lift one of the rested balls of dough and place it on your lightly-floured counter, skin side down. The ball will be rather flat and relaxed.

Pull the edges of the circle in towards the middle of the ball and pinch them together to form a tighter and smaller ball. Now turn the ball over, skin-side up.

Use your cupped hands to rotate the ball, rather like a steering wheel, at the same time skidding the dough across the work surface by moving your pinkies and the edges of your hands towards each other. The work surface should grip the bottom of the dough and you will notice how the skin becomes tighter as the ball firms up. Allow the skin to get quite taut but try not to burst it.

Place the loaf, skin-side down, in the middle of a floured couche. Fold the ends of the cloth over to cover the dough and place the dough in its round container.

Allow the dough to proof for two to four hours, depending on the temperature. Do the fingertip test described on page 94 to check whether the dough is fully proofed.

Baking

Heat the oven to 220 degrees Celsius. Place an empty steam pan on the lower shelf of the oven. Line a baking sheet with baking paper, baking spray or oil.

When the dough is ready, carefully tip the loaf/loaves upside down onto the baking tin. Score by cutting a large C or X on the top. When you feel more confident you could try a decorative spiral cut. Pour a cup of boiling water into the steam pan.

Place the loaf/loaves in the oven and bake for 30-45 minutes. After 20 minutes, check and turn if needed, to ensure even browning. If the loaf is already brown, turn the heat down to 200 -180 degrees Celsius.

The crust should be a deep burnished colour. If after 45 minutes you are in doubt, return the loaf to the oven for a further seven minutes. The crust might also have a few attractive bursts along the scored lines. These will give you a glimpse of the gluten threads just below the crust.

Cool the loaf/loaves on a rack for at least two hours. This bread's flavour develops remarkably over time. It is often at its best from day two onwards.

Tip for slicing a round loaf

Cut the first six slices from the one side of the loaf. Now place the loaf cut-side down and cut each slice from the crown to the base.

10

Rye
Bread

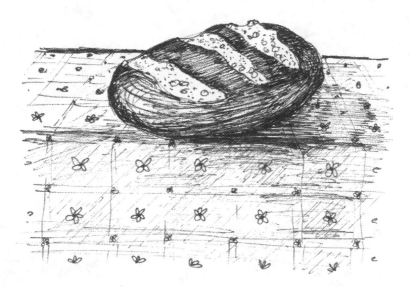

The first rye bread I ever had was pumpernickel, that dark, nearly black whole rye bread that the Dutch love to eat. I still have fond memories of the little French bakery in the centre of Cape Town where this bread was sold. It's the type of bread that grows on you, much like the taste of olives. A real delicacy, especially when served with slivers of smoked salmon or cumin cheese.

Two paper-thin slices are enough to fill you up. Working with rye flour takes quite a bit of practice. Rye dough lacks the elasticity and suppleness of wheat dough. At first it reminded me of working with clay, because it tends to stick to everything. The reason is that the proteins in rye differ from wheat proteins. Rye contains pentosan gums which interfere with gluten development. (See Chapter 6 for more information.) The typical light brown highly risen rye loaves commonly available on our shelves usually contain just a small percentage of rye flour. Often the dark colour of these loaves is attributable to food colouring.

A growing number of people prefer rye because they are sensitive to gluten. This is what convinced me to start experimenting with this grain. I soon discovered that sourdough fermentation enhances both the flavour and the handling of rye dough.

The first recipe below is my adaptation of Peter Reinhard's 100% rye sourdough. The loaf is compact and solid, with a dark crust full of small fermentation holes. It tastes like typical rye, and has the added advantage of keeping very well. A client of mine took some on a three-week hiking tour and it kept to the end of her trip!

Recipe for 100% sourdough rye bread

This recipe yields about 1 200 grams of dough. You could divide it into two loaves, or into one loaf plus a few bread rolls.

Suggested time schedule

It will take you two to three days to make this bread.

Day One: Feed your sourdough mother early in the morning. Mix the starter dough late in the afternoon or in the evening.

Day Two: Mix the dough early in the morning. Allow at least 4 hours for fermentation, 2 hours for proofing, and 30 to 60 minutes for baking. If you make an early start on Day Two, the bread could be ready for supper.

Recipe notes

> The recipe requires an active sourdough mother, last fed about 8 hours before you start. You could use your wheat sourdough mother, but if you plan to make rye regularly, I recommend that you convert your wheat mother to a rye mother simply by feeding her with rye flour.

> If you prefer a lighter rye, replace up to 50% of the rye flour with whole wheat or white bread flour.

> Caraway or aniseed is traditionally used to flavour rye bread. These could be omitted; many people prefer the natural rye flavour. Semolina can be used to decorate the crust.

Starter 1

120 g (160 ml) active sourdough mother

160 g (1 and 1/4 cup) rye flour

80 g/ml water

Measure the sourdough mother and water into your container. Stir together and add the rye flour. Mix well with a wooden spoon or dough scraper. Cover the bowl and allow to rest for 10 minutes.

Wet your one hand or your dough scraper and shape the dough into a ball. Knead it lightly while keeping your hand wet to limit the sticking. It should form a sticky, rough dough. Place it in a lightly oiled container and cover. Allow to ferment at room temperature for at least 4 hours or until doubled. Alternatively, depending on your baking schedule, refrigerate the starter overnight.

Starter 2

80 grams whole or cracked rye berries

140g /ml of water

Soak the grains in the water in a lidded container. Allow them to soften while the first starter develops.

Starter 1

Starter 2

220 g/ml water

450 g/3 ½ cups rye flour

15 g (1 tablespoon) salt

10 g (2 teaspoons) caraway seed (optional)

Making the dough

Remove the starters from the fridge one hour before making the dough.

Cut the first starter into a few smaller pieces and place them in a mixing bowl. Add the second starter and stir. Add the water, flour, salt and seeds and stir well to moisten all the dry ingredients. Cover the bowl and rest the dough for 10 to 30 minutes to allow all the moisture to be absorbed.

Sprinkle your counter with rye flour and turn out the dough. Keep a jug of water handy to moisten your hands. The dough should be wetter than baguette dough but drier than ciabatta dough. If it feels too dry, work in more water with your wet hands; if too wet, add small amounts of rye flour.

Handle the dough lightly with your fingertips. You will notice that it is not very elastic. Use a dough scraper to lift and turn it. Gentle kneading should take about 5 minutes.

Rest the dough on the counter and give it a few more turns. Place it in a clean lightly oiled container and cover. Ferment the dough for about 4 hours or until nearly doubled in size.

Dividing and shaping the dough

Sprinkle rye flour on your counter and turn out the dough. It should now be spongy and soft. Handle it as little as possible to avoid deflation.

Divide the dough as required. Pat the pieces into shape with floured hands and gently shape into rectangular loaves.

Place them in oiled or sprayed baking tins. I prefer to bake these loaves in traditional bread tins. 700 grams of dough fits comfortably into a 220 X 120 mm bread tin.

Lightly dust the tops of the loaves with a sprinkling of rye flour.

Slip the tins into plastic bags and proof for about 2 hours. Be careful not to over-proof the dough. The dough is ready when fine cracks appear on the surface.

Preheat the oven to 230 degrees Celsius and place an empty steam pan on the lower shelf. Sprinkle the tops of the loaves with semolina or seeds of your choice. Cut a slit down the middle of the crust with a pair of scissors.

Baking

Pour a cup of boiling water into the steam pan. Slide the baking tins into the oven and bake for 35 to 45 minutes, when the crusts should be dark brown. After 15 minutes, rotate the tins. If the crusts are dark already, turn down the heat to 180 degrees Celsius.

Cool the loaves on a rack for at least 2 hours before cutting.

You may like to look at the following 70% rye sourdough recipe that is available on the internet: http://www.thefreshloaf.com/node/13552/hansjoakim039s-favorite-70-sourdough-rye

http://www.thefreshloaf.com is one of my favourite bread websites and I can recommend it to fellow bakers who want to learn from passionate home bakers in the United States and elsewhere in the world.

11
Kitke
And Other Sacred Bread

"What is spiritual bread? The loaf in the oven. As a creature it bears the footprints of the Creator, and is that not spiritual enough?"

-Martin Versveld, Food for Thought

By now it will be clear to the reader that I consider all bread sacred. Nevertheless I prefer to use words like "holy" and "sacred" with caution. It is all too easy to slip into clichés or Biblical language when we talk about bread.

Nevertheless, it was a request for a "holy" bread that first introduced me to kitke. Panina, a fellow villager, wanted to place a standing order for kitke every Friday. Kitke, or challah, is the plaited loaf that Jewish families break on Fridays at the beginning of the Sabbath. The plaited shape reminds them of the twelve tribes of Israel, while the sprinkling of sesame or poppy seeds recalls the life-giving manna that fell from heaven.

As it happens, both my bread gurus, Reinhard and Glezer, are of Jewish descent and both of them have written about kitke. Maggie Glezer's book A Blessing of Bread: Recipes and Rituals, Memories and Mitzvahs is a treasure of a book in which she tells the compelling folk tales, histories and family stories of different Jewish communities, from Guatemala to Russia. There are photographs of the mothers and grandmothers who shared their traditions and recipes with her.

To begin with I made kitke by simply shaping my baguette dough into a three-stranded plait. This suited Panina as she and her daughter were both on an egg-free diet and kitke usually includes egg. After coming across Glezer's wonderful book, however, I had to try her challah. Her dough can be shaped into endless intriguing forms and it tastes great.

This type of bread makes a perfect gift for a special event. I often bake birthday breads for friends. Here is the message I sent to my friend Tracey with the gift bread I made for her.

Dearest Tracey

Your birthday has inspired me to make you a Kugelhopf, a traditional continental yeast cake of Austrian, German, Polish, Alsatian and Jewish origin.

It is rich in butter.

May your year be full of riches, both material and spiritual. Smooth, golden and "buttery".

It is avoured with rum-drenched fruit.

May all your senses be blessed with spices and aromas. Heady
avours all year round. Perhaps some travel to exotic destinations?

It has been given ample time to ferment and proof.

May you take the time to grow even more fully into your true Essence this year.

Take a bite and know how much I love you!

Bread-brother Niël's wedding loaf was a fantabulous construction – a giant oval babka. More than two kilogram of enriched dough filled with chocolate, hazelnuts and fruit. The filling was enfolded in two large strands lying side by side like two spooning lovers. I was unable to deliver the babka myself, because as it turned out my erstwhile partner in Passionate Bread-Making was getting married on the same day I was giving a bread-making workshop at the oven he had built for me in McGregor. So we lovingly wrapped the babka in tissue paper and bubble wrap, decorated it with lavender from the garden and added a card and a painting by Lies. It travelled to the Kamanassie homestead in Paul's Beetle, labelled "Wedding Bread" and with strict instructions to "Handle with Care" and "Keep This Side Up". Back home I could feel Bread Brother's presence at my shoulder throughout the workshop. When it came to scoring the dough and I took out his famous Le Sliceur to demonstrate the action, I noticed that it was exactly five o'clock, the moment when Niël would be marrying his Gabbi in the veld. That's if the bridegroom is on time, I thought with a secret smile.

The following recipe is based on Maggie Glezer's Czernowitzer challah, which was given to her by Lotte Lehman. This bread originated in Czernowitz, a city known in the late nineteenth century as the Vienna of Eastern Europe.

Kitke dough is usually enriched with eggs, butter and sugar. These ingredients slow down the action of yeast, hence the need to give the fermentation a kick-start with a yeast sponge before adding the heavier ingredients.

Czernowitzer Challah

This recipe yields about one kilogram of dough, which should allow for two large loaves or one large loaf and a few smaller rolls. It's a versatile recipe. For my popular sticky buns known as Gregorhagens, I roll out the dough in a large rectangular shape, top it with cinnamon, sugar and a layer of cake fruit, then roll it up like a Swiss roll and slice it into twelve rolls. I glaze them with egg wash and when they come from the oven I add a dollop of lemon icing before selling them as mock Danish buns at the market.

Time schedule

This bread can be made in 4 – 5 hours. Start by making the sponge. About twenty minutes later the sponge is added to the rest of the dough ingredients. Allow about 2 hours for fermentation. After shaping, proof the dough for a further 2 hours. Baking takes about 30 minutes. If necessary, the dough can be retarded in the fridge, either during the fermentation stage or once you have shaped the loaves. Take it out one hour before shaping or baking.

Yeast sponge

7 g (2 ¼ teaspoons) instant yeast

100g (¾ cup) white bread flour

170 g/ml lukewarm water

Mix all the ingredients until smooth. Allow the sponge to stand for about 15 minutes until it gets puffy.

Dough

2 large eggs

110 g (100 ml) sunflower oil

8 g (1 ½ teaspoon) salt

55 g (1/3 cup) granulated sugar

400 g (3 cups) white bread flour

1 egg for glazing

poppy or sesame seeds for garnishing (optional)

Whisk the eggs, oil, salt and sugar into the fermented sponge. Mix well until everything is incorporated. Gradually stir in the flour to form a rough dough. Cover the dough and rest it for 15 to 20 minutes.

Tip the dough out onto your counter and knead it for about 10 minutes. I find it easier to divide the dough in two and knead each piece separately until it is smooth and velvety. The dough should be firm and easy to handle. If it is too stiff, add a small amount of water by wetting your hands.

Fermenting the dough

Cover the dough and allow to rise for 2 hours, or until doubled in size.

Shaping and proofing the dough

Turn out the dough and divide according to your needs. Prepare two baking sheets with oil or baking paper to receive the shaped dough.

For a braided loaf, weigh the dough and divide into three equal pieces. Shape into rounds and allow them to rest skin-side down for about 5 minutes.

Sprinkle flour onto your work surface. Press each ball into a flat disk with your palm before rolling it out with a rolling pin into a very thin rectangular sheet. The shape doesn't matter too much, as long as the sheet is longer than the final length of your baking tin.

The next step is to tightly and evenly roll up each sheet into a sausage or strand. Then roll each sausage under your palms until it is smooth and even, much like the final step of rolling a baguette (see Chapter 7).

Lay the three strands next to each other on the work surface. Start plaiting in the middle of the strands and work towards you. Plait very loosely in order to leave space for the strands to expand during proofing. Pinch the bottom ends of the strands firmly together to seal the plait. Now turn the plait so that the loose ends face you. Plait the other half and seal the ends in the same way.

Lift the challah and gently put it on the prepared baking sheet. Slip the baking sheet into a large plastic bag. Proof for about two hours. The loaf should triple in size.

Baking

Preheat the oven to 180 degrees Celsius.

To prepare the glaze, beat the egg with a pinch of salt and one teaspoon of water. Brush the mixture on carefully without distorting the puffed up challah.

Bake the plaited loaves for 20 to 35 minutes until they colour an even brown. Turn the baking tin after 20 minutes to ensure even baking. At this point you could cover the top of the loaf with tin foil if the loaves are browning too fast. Cool on a rack before breaking the bread.

Saturday after the market.
The oven is still warm enough for
roasted veggies.

10.45 am

12

The Saturday Market – Bread for

BARTER

It is Saturday morning. By half past seven I have sorted and packed all the bread in baskets, ready for the market. I'm loading the car when two impatient customers arrive at our gate.

"Ve vent to zee market, end der vas nozink!"

"No," I explain," the market only starts at nine o'clock. But do come inside; you can buy your bread here."

They select their loaves, then give us a hand, and soon we're on our way down Voortrekker Street.

There is already a buzz of activity on the street corner. Bruce and Di are unpacking their vegetables, jams and olive oils onto a trestle table. Janet has arrived with her pies, quiches, cakes and biscuits. Judy has a boot full of veggies. Two little girls are all set to sell their muffins from a red doll's table. One of them is saving up for a piano. The regulars start pitching up. They help us take our folding table from the boot. Lies covers it with a colourful ethnic cloth before the bread baskets are lifted from the car. A table full of bounty.

Check: money box, tissue wrappers. Yes, we are ready to trade.

In no time we are surrounded by people – old acquaintances, complete strangers, visitors from the city. The bread literally flies off the table. By now I know more or less who wants what, and some people have regular orders. Locals bring their own bags or baskets; for the rest, we wrap the loaves in squares of paper as Lies used to do as a child.

The McGregor morning market is the weekly highlight on the village calendar. It may be the shortest market in the world – all over within an hour – but then people continue to chat up and down the street in little buzz groups. I love to see them walking off with their loaves. There's Pasquelina, newly arrived from the Netherlands after buying a house in the village. And there's Ray with his tartan peak over his long grey ponytail. We had to disappoint him today: no raisin bread left. I made a mental note to bake more of those next week. As I put our table back in the boot I spot Mike Kamstra in serious conversation with Paul. They gesticulate with expansive gestures, their wrapped sourdough loaves in their hands.

✦

On 8 April 2006 we celebrated the centenary of the naming of our village. After first being called Lady Grey, the name was changed to McGregor on this day in 1906 because a town named Lady Grey already existed. Siegfried, owner of the guest house across the road from us, came up with the bright suggestion that all stall holders should wear festive hats for the occasion.

As we set up our tables that morning, the cameras started clicking. What was McGregor up to now? Siegfried was there in a bright orange overall and mink Cossack hat. Connie wore a full bee-keeper's outfit, complete with protective headgear. I wore a green silk gown with top hat while Lies was in a flowing African caftan. The slogan on her bright red beret explained it all: "Our town McGregor = 100".

The market was busier than usual that day. Chris sold organic veggies. Connie and Alan offered cheese and pesto. Siegfried, who had wheeled his ball-and-claw table all the way from his front door on Voortrekker Street, displayed a stylish cake stand with finely crafted pastries, milk tarts and pâtés. The table was a work of art.

Last but not least came my bread table. Baskets bursting with Karoo loaves, baguettes, ciabattas and 100% rye. Focaccias filled with blue cheese and walnuts. And the novelty of the day – Gregorhagens, our own version of scrumptious Copenhagens. Visitors were astonished at the variety. It was hard to believe, they said, that such delicacies could still be found outside Woollies.

At ten o'clock quiet descended on the street. We started to pack up our baskets, rather sad to leave the festivities behind. So we started bartering with left-over products. The farmers handed out bunches of spinach in return for the last of the bread. Connie offered cubes of farmer's Gouda from her tasting board. On the spur of the moment I broke a baguette to go with the cheese. Siegfried opened a liver pate and we scooped it from the jar with pieces of broken bread. Chris contributed crisp lettuce and radishes and before long it had turned into a spontaneous street picnic. A few late-coming customers joined us in sharing the fruits of the bounteous valley.

Lies and Anthony became locked in a discussion on the economy and the striking textile workers. Our own factories were closing; it was cheaper to import clothing from China, where workers labour for a bowl of rice, or maybe a bicycle.

"In the final analysis," said Anthony, "every sale is simply an exchange between people."

I'm busy packing up the table. All that's left are empty baskets and a few breadcrumbs. Around me I see waving hands, talking mouths and shiny eyes. This too is an exchange; an interchange of energies between people. Again I feel part of a long and ancient tradition.

Paper and coins for two days of work: money to buy food and flour for the week ahead.

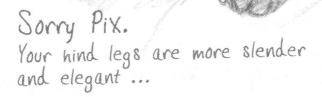

Sorry Pix.
Your hind legs are more slender
and elegant ...

Friend. Peacemaker. Nature lover.
Lover of life and food. Protector. Mate.

13

Definition of
terms

A

Autolyse
A resting period of 10 to 30 minutes after flour and water have been mixed. The flour hydrates and its gluten develops, before yeast and salt are added. The resting period cuts down on the amount of kneading required.

B

Babka
A rich festive loaf from the Jewish tradition. Babka means "grandmother" in Polish.

B

Baguette
A traditional long French loaf

C

Challah
A plaited Sabbath loaf from the Jewish Ashkenazi tradition. (See kitke.)

Ciabatta
Italian flat bread with typically large fermentation holes. The Italian name literally means "slipper".

Commercial yeast
Saccaramyces cerevisiae is a form of live yeast which is available as fresh yeast, active dried yeast, and instant yeast. It is more potent than yeast which occurs naturally in the atmosphere. Most recipes in this book call for instant yeast which is available in sealed 10 gram foil packets. It is advisable to discard a packet once it has been opened.

F

Fermentation

The process that gives bread its characteristic flavour. Yeast feeds on the carbohydrates in flour and releases carbon dioxide. The resulting air bubbles stretch the gluten and give bread its airy texture.

Foccaccia

Italian flatbread topped or filled with cheese, herbs or olives. Derived from the Italian focus, which means oven.

G

Gluten

Gluten is derived from a special combination of proteins found in wheat. It forms a network of fine elastic threads when flour is mixed with water. The gluten strands retain the air bubbles in dough and make it possible for dough to be stretched and shaped.

Gluten window test

A test for determining whether gluten has developed sufficiently after a period of kneading. A piece of stretched dough is held up against the light. If it rips easily it needs further kneading, but if it forms an even transparent sheet, the gluten is well developed.

K

Kitke

A plaited loaf for special Jewish holidays. The South African name for challah.

R

Rising of dough

The first rise occurs directly after the mixing and kneading of dough and takes between one and four hours, depending on the type of dough and the temperature.

The second rise, or proofing period, happens once the dough has been divided and shaped.

The final rise, also known as oven spring, takes place in the oven.

S

Sourdough mother or sourdough culture

A sourdough culture colonised by natural yeast spores, Saccaramyces exiguus, as well as lactobacilli and other bacteria. This culture is used for fermenting sourdough bread.

Starter dough

A quantity of already fermented dough that is added to a new dough to kick-start the process. The starter is left for a period (often overnight) to ferment before being incorporated into the final dough. A starter dough improves the taste, texture and longevity of bread. A starter dough can be made either with sourdough or with commercial yeast.

There are three types of starter dough. Poolish is sloppy, containing more or less equal quantities of water and flour; biga is firm; and pâte fermentée is dough retained from an earlier bake.

Measurements

A few commonly used weights and measurements

1 cup of flour = 130 g

1/2 cup of flour = 65 grams

1/4 cup of flour = 30 grams

1 cup of water = *180 ml = 180 gram*

3/4 cup of water = 120 ml = 120 grams

1/2 cup of water = 80 ml = 80 grams

1/4 cup of water = 40 ml = 40 grams

2/3 cup of water = 60 ml = 60 grams

1/3 cup of water = 30 ml = 30 grams

15

Bibliography

Nancy Silverton, *Breads from the La Brea Bakery*. Villard Books, Random House, Inc., New York. 1996.

Maggie Glezer, *Artisan Baking Across America*. Artisan, New York. 2000.

Maggie Glezer, *A Blessing of Bread. Recipes and Rituals, Memories and Mitzvahs*. Artisan, New York. 2004.

Peter Reinhart, *The Bread Baker's Apprentice*. Ten Speed Press, Berkeley, California. 2001.

Allan Scott & Daniel Wing, *The Bread Builders. Hearth Loaves and Masonry Ovens*. Chelsea Green Publishing. 1999.

Lise Boily, Jean-Francois Blanchette, *The Bread Ovens of Quebec*. National Museums of Canada, 1997.

Het Nieuwe Handboek voor de Broodbakkery door "Quidam". Uitgave van die NV Uitgevers – Maatschappij AE Kluwer – Deventer.

Dine van Zyl, *Boerekos. Tradisionele Suid-Afrikaanse Resepte*. Human en Rousseau. 1985

Elizabeth David, *English Bread and Yeast Cookery*. Allen Lane, Penquin Books Ltd., London. 1977.

16

Builders of bread
ovens

1. Niël Jonker assists you in building your own brick oven, according to the plans of Alan Scott to whom Niël apprenticed in the USA.

Buy Alan's book 'The bread builders', to do it yourself, or contact Lela Scott in California for their commercial sized oven plans:

lilarscott@yahoo.com   www.ovencrafters.net

Niël also hosts bread workshops at his 'Beeeg Baardskeerdersbos Bakoond' monthly:

info @nieljonker.co.za www.nieljonker.co.za

2. Peter Savage builds earth ovens in Gauteng:

petesavage@mweb.co.za 0828760276

3. Shimmy Perap builds excellent brick ovens and has tried his hand at Alan Scott's plans for De Oude Bakkerij in Stellenbosch:

021 5593820 pizzaovenallbake@telkomsa.net

http://www.pizzaovensallbakeoven.co.za

17

Index